FRANK LANGELLA'S CYRANO

an adaptation of
Edmond Rostand's
CYRANO DE
BERGERAC

BROADWAY PLAY PUBLISHING INC
56 E 81st St., NY NY 10028-0202
212 772-8334 fax: 212 772-8358
http://www.BroadwayPlayPubl.com

FRANK LANGELLA'S CYRANO
© Copyright 1999 by Frank Langella

First printing: May 1999
ISBN: 0-88145-149-5

Book design: Marie Donovan
Word processing: Microsoft Word for Windows
Typographic controls: Xerox Ventura Publisher 2.0 P E
Typeface: Palatino
Copy editing: Liam Brosnahan
Printed on recycled acid-free paper and bound in the U S A.

PREFACE

To attempt CYRANO DE BERGERAC with a cast of a dozen people presents a host of traps—and I fell into about all of them. Some I pulled myself out of, and others swallowed me alive.

In this preface, I will try to describe to future pioneers the territory as I discovered it. After you have charted my course, you must chart your own and live with the consequences.

Consequences, by the way, I still feel are well worth risking. And I encourage anyone who wishes to test his mettle to take the trip.

As an actor I've played Cyrano twice before, in 1971 and 1980, at the Williamstown Theater Festival in Massachusetts. Both productions were essentially the same—huge cast, including hundreds of soldiers and hordes of nuns, grand costumes, quaint music; and both were very long.

Both were immensely successful with audiences and critics, and given the limited budgets and time constraints at Williamstown, all-out spectacles.

A number of years ago, it began to occur to me that this play, so universally loved, might be very effective as a chamber piece. My reasons were two-fold. Most of us have known the pain of unrequited love, and many people ruin their lives holding out for an ideal beyond them, when true happiness is right under their noses, so to speak.

What if all the pomp and ceremony were stripped away? The extraneous characters gone? All sense of period eliminated? Wouldn't a timeless love story remain? A tragic triangle for all time—and would it not perhaps be more tragic viewed in the simplest of settings, free from the frills and feathers of its day?

Secondly, I saw it as a production one could do anywhere—at any theater with a limited budget, and as a show easy to travel. And, of course, the character of Cyrano himself is a great ride for any actor. I had expressed the idea to Todd Haimes of the Roundabout Theater one year. He said, "Do it". So, I sat down and began to adapt my favorite translation, the Brian Hooker.

As I began, I realized I had been editing the play in my head for years—for the form it now exists in took shape fairly quickly. At first I cut too much, then over-restored, then over-cut again. I will not recount here the dozens of versions I created and discarded over the year or even the dozens of changes made during rehearsals and a desperately needed long preview in New York.

The version herein contained is the one we played at the Roundabout and it is meant to convey the heart and soul of Cyrano's story. It was arrived at, at no little cost to a patient and courageous group of actors who had to survive my constant changes as adaptor and director; as well as another actor playing Cyrano during a large portion of rehearsal, while I stumbled through those changes.

I can best serve the next adventurer by trying to describe some of the mistakes I made.

First, the physical production. It had been my original intention to do as bare-bones a production as possible. A unit set of various levels easily workable as a theater hall, or a camp, or a garden, etc. I also envisioned costumes of utmost simplicity—clean lines, soft easy flow for the women; hard, strong, lean for the men— but somewhere in the early stages, I veered away from that concept and, again with the constant devotion of my designers, began to create an ersatz period look that resulted in a mock-romantic style, neither spectacle, nor elegant simplicity—but rather a sense of a watered-down period piece. I would urge future productions to keep it extremely simple. Bare-bones set and costumes. No hint of any era. Also, make your scene changes swift and simple—allow the characters to carry you from one scene to the next—not the stagehands.

The music too was a demon. I tried 40's love songs, Duke Ellington jazz and some over-sentimental classical. All of it unsuccessful. I tend to think little or no music would best serve this version.

Cyrano removed from the era in which he was written can seem, if the actor and the production are not vigilant, like an over-florid animated Hallmark Card. Stripped of the standards and mores of his day, his pain and longing can look dangerously silly. It's only in the depth of feeling and honesty of performing that a sense of semi-classical pretentiousness can be avoided.

On the plus side, in the acting, I encouraged a total lack of what I had come to regard as "that sound"—a sort of fake semi-classical acting noise that passes for seriousness of intent—nor did I want the modern, moment to moment, sub-realism that results in actors sounding so with it as to be past it. The company worked tirelessly and exhaustively toward that end—and suffered through endless variations of that theme; at various times performing at breathless speed,

in the dark, improvising, and—at one glorious
afternoon rehearsal—in Spanish. Efforts were made
to break away from a traditional grandiose attitude
toward this material, and play the characters with a
full-out honesty, truth, and simplicity—not losing their
passion or power.

Roxane is best served in this version as a young
woman who learns about herself as the play progresses.
At first in love with love and Christian's beauty, then
the realization of her shallowness and her eagerness
to mature and finally, in her loss, a quiet acceptance
culminating in a genuine rage at her betrayal.

Christian is not a dolt—but an honest, upright,
honorable man—full of real love and with a sweet
understanding of his shortcomings—just because
he can't talk to a woman doesn't mean in all other
respects he isn't a fine and decent man who rises to
great nobility when he learns the truth and forces
Cyrano to tell Roxane.

And so on—Marguerite is a fine woman, not a
dithering matron. Le Bret, a good friend—solid and
true, Ragueneau, a gentle sometime poet. DeGuiche,
not a boring stuffed shirt, but a shrewd and intelligent
politician. And Lise is here conceived as a young
woman deeply in love with Cyrano—silent throughout,
hoping that one day he will turn to see, that while he
has been languishing over his own unrequited love—
she has been there always, hoping he will see her,
which he never does.

And Cyrano is himself not altogether a noble character,
but fearful and cowardly and using his nose as the
reason he will not act upon his true desires—as many
people often use anything to keep from acting on their
dreams. To that point, I would suggest the actor
playing Cyrano be a relatively young man, since part

of Cyrano's self-deception should come from his youth and inexperience.

It is then in this version, a small village of people—all interconnected and interdependent—and the deeply intimate unfolding of a tragedy, of which they are all aware that should hold the audience—not spectacle. Taking Cyrano out of his era is dangerous—but playing this version with total conviction and honest intentions is ultimately rewarding. It is often said that all the characters are stick figures, there to serve Cyrano's shining star. This version, by its very simplicity, avoids that cliché. Each of the characters is a clear and specific individual aware of and party to Cyrano's story, and they became rewarding to play.

Finally, my production, it could be said charitably, was a noble failure. The New York critics, with a few exceptions, were dismissive and at times vicious in their denouncement of me and my concept. Lack of approval cannot stop you. Do what you want to do. Ignore my advice here even, and follow *your* instinct.

Risk this Cyrano. It is, I hope, full of his soul and yearning and it was, for my soul, a rewarding and thrilling journey—one I envy you, should you decide to go for it.

F L

ACKNOWLEDGEMENTS

There was nothing but encouragement and help from the following people and I thank them all. Todd Haimes and Ellen Richard for giving me the hall. Trent Jones and Jeremiah Coyle for their able and tireless assistance. Ray Virta for playing Cyrano exhaustively through rehearsals. Designers James Noone, Carrie Robbins, and Marc B Weiss for their flexibility. Stage Managers Jay Adler and John Handy for patience and fortitude. Casting director Jim Carnahan for his care and concern. Steve White and Armand Schultz for fighting with me. Richard Nelson and Jerry Zaks for coming to early previews and offering advice. Whoopi, for putting up endlessly with the phrase, "What do you think of...?" And finally, to each and every member of the company for their constant great spirits, humor, talent, and devotion. Never once did I feel anything but deep loyalty and commitment to an ideal that often, in my own mind, wavered. They were the real heroes of this CYRANO, and I am forever in their debt.

ORIGINAL PRODUCTION

CYRANO premiered at the Roundabout Theater
Company on 9 December 1997. The cast and creative
contributors were:

CHRISTIAN . . . . .Marcus Chait
ROXANE . . . . Allison Mackie
MARGUERITE . . . . Mikel Sarah Lambert
RAGUENEAU . . . . Terry Alexander
LISE . . . . Lisa Leguillou
LE BRET . . . . George Morfogen
DE GUICHE . . . . Shawn Elliot
MONTFLEURY . . . . .Adam LeFevre
CYRANO . . . . Frank Langella
VALVERT . . . . Armand Schultz
CARBON . . . . .Rod McLachlan
PRIEST . . . . Brian Keane
SOLDIER . . . . Jeffrey Cox

Understudies:
CYRANO . . . . Ray Virta
LE BRET, DE GUICHE, & CARBON . . . . Timothy Wheeler
ROXANE, LISE, & MARGUERITE . . . . .Teri Lamm
RAGUENEAU & MONTFLEURY . . . . Brian Keane
CHRISTIAN, VALVERT, & PRIEST . . . . .Jeffrey Cox

Director/adaptor .... Frank Langella
Set design .... James Noone
Costume design .... Carrie Robbins
Lighting design .... Marc B Weiss
Sound design .... Laura Grace Brown
Fight director .... J Steven White
Prosthetics design .... Matthew W Mungle
Translation .... Brian Hooker

CHARACTERS

ROXANE, *a beauty*
CHRISTIAN, *handsome*
MARGUERITE, *a matron*
RAGUENEAU, *a pastry cook*
LISE, *a servant girl, mute*
LE BRET, *best friend to* CYRANO
DE GUICHE, *a politician*
MONTFLEURY, *a bad actor*
CYRANO, *a poet*
VALVERT, *a peacock*
CARBON, *a good captain*
PRIEST, *a simple mind*
SOLDIER, *a young man with a flute*

Note: the actors playing VALVERT *and the* PRIEST *double as soldiers in ACT TWO, Scene One*

SETTING

ACT ONE

ACT TWO

ACT ONE

Scene One

(A Hall)

(The house lights fade, music. ROXANE enters the box. Across the theater CHRISTIAN enters. Their eyes meet. MARGUERITE enters behind ROXANE and ushers her out. CHRISTIAN goes to the box, places a white rose down. RAGUENEAU enters, meets CHRISTIAN in front of the stage. Music fades.)

RAGUENEAU: Where's the lady?

CHRISTIAN: She's always here. I must find some way of meeting her. I am dying of love. And you know everyone—the whole town. You put them all into your songs. At least you can tell me her name.

RAGUENEAU: I am going.

CHRISTIAN: No—wait! I can't talk to a woman. I have no wit. This fine manner of speaking and of writing nowadays—not for me! I am a soldier—and afraid.

RAGUENEAU: The play begins at eight. There's time, I'll stay a little. Lise? Where is that woman?

(LISE enters.)

RAGUENEAU: Lise, give me some wine. There should be a full house tonight, I'll expect a handsome profit.

(She pours out wine for him from a service tray around her neck. LE BRET enters.)

LE BRET: Ragueneau, have you seen Cyrano?

RAGUENEAU: Not today. Oh...Le Bret. This is Christian de Neuvillette. Just arrived.

CHRISTIAN: Yes, I've been here two or three weeks only. I join the Guards tomorrow.

LE BRET: Good luck. Cyrano's not here? Thank God.

CHRISTIAN: Why so?

LE BRET: Why?—Montfleury is playing tonight.

CHRISTIAN: What's that to him?

RAGUENEAU: Cyrano hates Montfleury so much, he has forbidden him to appear on the stage for three weeks.

CHRISTIAN: Well?

RAGUENEAU: Montfleury plays!—

CHRISTIAN: Yes—what then?

LE BRET: Ah! That is what I came to see.

CHRISTIAN: This Cyrano—who is he?

RAGUENEAU: He is the man with the long sword. He's in the Guards. You'll meet him.

LE BRET: An extraordinary man. The best friend, and the bravest soul alive.

RAGUENEAU: And such a remarkable appearance! He will not come.

LE BRET: Oh, won't he? I'll keep searching.

(LE BRET *moves off, still looking.* ROXANE *appears, followed by* MARGUERITE, *her guardian. She carries the white rose. She sits in the box, taking no notice of* CHRISTIAN.)

CHRISTIAN: *(Sees* ROXANE*)* There! Quick! Look!—there— in the box!—

RAGUENEAU: Herself?

CHRISTIAN: What's her name?

RAGUENEAU: Roxane.

CHRISTIAN: Ah!—Roxane.

RAGUENEAU: Unmarried...

CHRISTIAN: Oh!—

RAGUENEAU: An orphan... She's Cyrano's cousin... the man we spoke of just now.

(DE GUICHE *enters the box, followed by* VALVERT. *He whispers to* ROXANE.)

CHRISTIAN: And the man?...

RAGUENEAU: Oho! That man?... De Guiche...in love with her...married himself, however. Wants Roxane, therefore, to marry Valvert, that other fellow...friend of his, excellent swordsman, somewhat melancholy... but...well, agreeable!...She says no...nevertheless, De Guiche persists, he's powerful...not above persecuting... I have written a little song about his little game. Should make him furious.

(ROXANE *is now watching* CHRISTIAN.)

RAGUENEAU: Very well, you have the news. I'll be leaving you...Lise, go to the shop when you have finished here.

CHRISTIAN: Ragueneau, wait! Please stay with me.

RAGUENEAU: Not I. There's a bar not far away and I am dying of thirst. Besides, I hate the theater. Too much bad acting.

(RAGUENEAU'S *eyes travel from* CHRISTIAN *to* ROXANE *and back again.*)

RAGUENEAU: She's looking at you.

CHRISTIAN: Roxane!...

RAGUENEAU: Don't you want to hear my song? Very well, then. I'll be leaving you. Goodnight. Goodnight. *(He goes.)*

(LE BRET reenters, just missing RAGUENEAU's exit.)

LE BRET: Ragueneau gone? I must tell you something—he's a good friend of yours?—

CHRISTIAN: Yes!

LE BRET: Well, he's as good as dead—understand? He wrote a song about—it doesn't matter. I've just learned there's a hundred men waiting for him tonight—

CHRISTIAN: A hundred? Where are they to be?

LE BRET: The Great Bridge. On his way home. Tell him so. Save his life. Cyrano will come! I must stay here. There may be trouble!

CHRISTIAN: Yes, but where am I to find him?

LE BRET: Go to the bars. Find him. Warn him.

CHRISTIAN: I will. God, what swine—a hundred against one man? I must save him.

(Looks at ROXANE—she at him—tears himself away)

DE GUICHE: Begin the play!

(The lights change, three raps are heard, music.)

MONTFLEURY: "Thrice happy he who hides from pomp and power in sylvan shade or solitary bower; Where balmy zephyrs fan his burning cheeks—"

A VOICE: *(From the back of the house)* Stop. Have I not forbidden you these three weeks?

LE BRET: Cyrano!

THE VOICE: *(Moving about the house)* King of clowns! Leave the stage—at once!

MONTFLEURY: "Thrice happy he who hides from..."

THE VOICE: Well? Well? Well?... Must I come up there and pluck that forest from your shoulders?

MONTFLEURY: *(In a voice increasingly feeble)* "Thrice happy he..."

THE VOICE: Go!!! *(Now in the center of the house)* I begin to grow angry!

MONTFLEURY: Gentlemen, if you protect me—

DE GUICHE: Well—proceed!

CYRANO: Fly goose! Shoo! Take to your wings.

DE GUICHE: See here—

CYRANO: Off stage!!

DE GUICHE: One moment—

CYRANO: What! You're still there? Very well—then— I enter—left—with knife—to carve this large Italian sausage.

MONTFLEURY: Sir, I will not permit you to insult me in this manner.

CYRANO: Oh! What manner would you prefer? Attend to me—full moon! I clap my hands, three times—At the third you will eclipse yourself. Ready? One!

MONTFLEURY: I—I really think....

CYRANO: Two!

MONTFLEURY: Perhaps I had better—

CYRANO: Three!

MONTFLEURY: After all, sir, what reason have you to hate me so much? I'm just an actor.

CYRANO: My dear sir...that's reason enough!

MONTFLEURY: But you'll close the play—and the money—do you expect me to return it?

CYRANO: You speak your first word of intelligence!
I will not wound the mantle of the muse— There's your
money, catch! *(Throws him a sack of coins)*

MONTFLEURY: But sir, I have a duty to my audience—

CYRANO: And hold your tongue. *(Coming down to the
foot of the stage)* Or tell me, why are you staring at my
nose! Does it astonish you?

MONTFLEURY: No, you misunderstand my—

CYRANO: Is it long and soft and dangling like a trunk?

MONTFLEURY: I have not said—

CYRANO: Or crooked, like an owl's beak?

MONTFLEURY: I—

CYRANO: Perhaps a pimple ornaments the end of it?

MONTFLEURY: No!—

CYRANO: Or a fly parading up and down?

MONTFLEURY: I have been careful not to look.

CYRANO: And why not, if you please?

MONTFLEURY: Why—

CYRANO: It disgusts you, then?

MONTFLEURY: My dear sir—

CYRANO: Possibly you find it just a trifle large?

MONTFLEURY: Oh no!—small, very small,
infinitesimal—

CYRANO: What? How? You accuse me of absurdity?
Small—my nose? Why—

MONTFLEURY: My God—

CYRANO: *(Coming onto the stage, we see him fully for the
first time.)* Magnificent, my nose!... You pug, you knob,
you button head. Know that I glory in this nose of mine,

for a great nose indicates a great man. Whilst that face,
that blank inglorious concavity—is as devoid of pride,
of poetry, of soul, of picturesqueness, of contour, of
character, of nose, in short—as that which at the end
of that limp spine of yours—my left foot... *(He kicks*
MONTFLEURY *in the rear.)*

MONTFLEURY: Help me, sirs! Help me!

DE GUICHE: This man is growing tiresome.

VALVERT: Yes, he blows his trumpet!

DE GUICHE: Well—will no one interfere?

VALVERT: No one? Watch, I'll put him in his place.
(To CYRANO*)* Ah...your nose, ahem!...your nose is...
rather large!

CYRANO: Rather—

VALVERT: Oh well—

CYRANO: Is that all?

VALVERT: Well, of course—

CYRANO: Ah no, young man! You are too simple.
Why, you might have said a great many things!
My God, why waste your opportunity? For example,
thus:—*Aggressive*: I, sir, if that nose were mine, I'd have
it amputated—on the spot! *Friendly*: How do you drink
with such a nose? You ought to have a cup made
specially. *Descriptive*: 'Tis a rock—a crag—a cape—
a cape? Say rather, a peninsula! *Inquisitive*: What is that
receptacle—A razor-case or a portfolio? *Kindly*: Ah,
do you love the little birds so much that when they
come and sing to you, you give them this to perch on?
Insolent: Sir, when you smoke, the neighbors must
suppose your chimney is on fire. *Cautious*: Take care—a
weight like that might make you topheavy. *Thoughtful*:
Somebody fetch my parasol—those delicate colors fade
so in the sun! *Pedantic*: Does not Aristophanes mention

a mythologic monster called Hippocampelephant-
ocamelos? Surely we have here the original! *Eloquent*:
When it blows, the typhoon howls, and the clouds
darken. *Dramatic*: When it bleeds—The Red Sea!
Enterprising: What a sign for some perfumer! *Lyric*:
Hark—the horn of Roland calls to summon
Charlemagne! *Simple*: When do they unveil the
monument? *Rustic*: Hey? What? Call that a nose?
Na na—I ain't no fool like what you think I be—that
there's a blue cucumber! *Military*: Point against cavalry!
Practical: Why not a lottery with this for the grand
prize? Or, *literary*: Was this the nose that launched a
thousand ships? These, my dear sir, are things you
might have said had you some tinge of letters or of wit
to color your remarks. But wit—not so, you never had
an atom—and of letters, you need but three to write
you down—A...S...S.

DE GUICHE: Valvert—come.

(VALVERT *comes out of the box onto the stage.*)

VALVERT: Oh—these arrogant grand airs!—A clown
who—look at him—just a silly poet—an average
soldier! No honors on his chest.

CYRANO: I carry my honors on my soul, shining there
for me alone. I go caparisoned in gems unseen, trailing
white plumes of freedom, garlanded with my good
name.

VALVERT: Dolt, bumpkin, fool, insolent dog, jobbernowl!

CYRANO: Ah, yes? And I—Hercule-Savinien de Cyrano
de Bergerac!

VALVERT: Egocentric buffoon!

CYRANO: Oh!

VALVERT: Well, what now?

CYRANO: I must do something to relieve these cramps—This is what comes of lack of exercise—Ah!

VALVERT: What is all this?

CYRANO: My sword has gone to sleep.

VALVERT: *(Draws his sword)* So be it!

CYRANO: You shall die exquisitely.

VALVERT: Poet!

CYRANO: Why yes, a poet, as you say. So, while we fence, I'll compose, just for you, an extemporaneous poem.

VALVERT: A poem?

CYRANO: Yes. You know what that is?

VALVERT: Oh, come now...You—

CYRANO: I'll compose one, while I fight with you, and at the end of the last line—thrust home!

VALVERT: Will you?

CYRANO: I will.

(VALVERT advances.)

CYRANO: Stop... *(Closes his eyes for an instant)* Let me choose my rhymes...Now! Here we go— *(He suits the action to the sword.)* Here by this stage we cannot stay, Give us a bit of light in the hall!

(Lights up in house)

CYRANO: Now I can see where'er you stray, So out, swords, and to work withal!

(The swords cross—the fight is on. The fight takes place in the theater up and down the aisles.)

CYRANO: A Lancelot, in his lady's hall... A Spartacus, at the Hippodrome!...

I dally awhile with you, dear jackal,
Then, as I end the refrain, thrust home!

Where shall I skewer my peacock?...Nay,
Better for you to have shunned this brawl!—

Here, in your heart? Should I let it stay?
In the belly, under your bladder...gall?

Hark, how the steel rings musical!
Mark how my point floats, light as the foam,

Ready to drive you back to the wall,
Then as I end the refrain, thrust home!

*(They disappear from sight for a time. We hear only the clash of swords—*VALVERT *reappears exhausted.* CYRANO *strolls back in.)*

CYRANO: Oh, for a rhyme!... You are white as whey—
You break, you cower, you cringe, you...crawl!

Tac!—and I parry your last essay;
So may the turn of a hand forestall

Life with its honey, death with its pall;
So may the turn of my fancy roam

Free, for a while, till the rhymes recall,
Then, as I end the refrain, thrust home!

(A silence) (Refrain)

CYRANO: Young man! Pray God, that is Lord of all,
Pardon your soul, for your time has come!

Beat—pass—fling you aslant, asprawl
Then, as I end the refrain...

(They have fought their way into the box.)

MONTFLUERY: Oh! *(A great cry)*

CYRANO: *(To* MONTFLEURY*)* Shush! *(To* VALVERT*)*
—Thrust home!

DE GUICHE: Valvert, come away.

(DE GUICHE *helps the wounded* VALVERT *off.*
MONTFLEURY *follows.*)

MONTFLUERY: What a scandal!

CYRANO: I have finished the poem, you may close
the lights! (*Lights fade in house. He finds the white rose*
ROXANE *dropped in the box.*)

LE BRET: Cyrano—come here and tell me...

CYRANO: Presently—

LE BRET: Do you know whom you have just offended?

CYRANO: No!

LE BRET: His name is De Guiche, a cold and calculating
man. Certain to succeed, and you have wounded his
protege.

CYRANO: De Guiche—what ostentation. Well, he's gone
now. Everyone's gone! Let's stay awhile.

LE BRET: Shall we dine?

CYRANO: Dine? No!

LE BRET: Why not?

CYRANO: Because—because I have no money.

LE BRET: But—the money you flung away?

CYRANO: Farewell, my paltry pension!

LE BRET: So you have, until the first of next month—?

CYRANO: Nothing.

LE BRET: What a fool!—

CYRANO: But—what a gesture!

(*They sit at the edge of the stage. He places the white rose*
down next to him. LISE, *who has been watching the events in*

rapt attention, comes to CYRANO, *offering her tray of food and wine.)*

CYRANO: My dear young woman, I cannot accept such a kindness— But, for fear that I may give you pain if I refuse, I will take, oh, not very much! A grape...one only! And a glass of water...and half a macaroon!

LE BRET: Old idiot! Thank you, Lise!

CYRANO: Oh, one thing more—

(She turns back to him.)

CYRANO: —your hand to kiss. *(He does so.)* Beautiful downcast eyes!... So shy...

(She drifts away.)

CYRANO: There now, Dinner!— *(—the macaroon)* Drink!— *(—the glass of water)* Dessert! *(—the grape)* God, I was hungry! Thank you.

(LISE goes to a corner, lingers to listen as she pretends to tidy her tray)

CYRANO: Well?

LE BRET: Where is this behavior leading you? What's your plan?

CYRANO: I have been wandering—wasting my force upon too many plans. Now I have chosen one.

LE BRET: What one?

CYRANO: The simplest. To make myself in all things admirable.

LE BRET: I see! Well, then, the real reason why you hate Montfleury—Come on, tell me.

CYRANO: That fool, who can't even hold his belly in his arms, still dreams of being sweetly dangerous with women—I hate him ever since one day he dared smile at—Oh, my friend, it was as if I had seen a huge snail crawling over some innocent flower.

LE BRET: How, what? Is it possible?—

CYRANO: For me to love?... I love.

LE BRET: May I know? You have never said—

CYRANO: Whom I love? Think a moment. Think of me—me, whom the plainest woman would despise— Me with this nose of mine that marches on before me by a quarter of an hour. Whom should I love? Why— of course—it must be the woman in the world most beautiful.

LE BRET: Most beautiful?

CYRANO: In all this world—most sweet; also most wise; most witty; and most fair!

LE BRET: Who and what is this woman?

CYRANO: Dangerous mortally, without meaning; exquisite without imagining. Nature's own snare to allure manhood. A white rose wherein love lies in ambush. Who knows her smile has known a perfect thing. She creates grace in her own image, brings heaven to earth in one movement of her hand.

LE BRET: Oh, well—of course, that makes everything clear!

CYRANO: Transparently.

LE BRET: Roxane—your cousin?

CYRANO: Yes; Roxane.

LE BRET: And why not? If you love her, tell her so.

CYRANO: My old friend—look at me, and tell me how much hope remains for me with this protuberance! I have no illusions! Now and then, I may grow tender, walking alone in the blue cool of evening, through

some garden fresh with flowers after the benediction
of the rain; my poor, big devil of a nose inhales April...
and so I follow with my eyes where some boy, with a
girl upon his arm, passes a patch of silver...and I feel
somehow, I wish I had a woman too, walking with little
steps under the moon, and holding my arm so, and
smiling. Then I dream—and I forget...And then I see
the shadow of my profile on the wall! I have my bitter
days, knowing myself so ugly, so alone. Sometimes—

LE BRET: You weep?

CYRANO: Weep! Oh, no, not that, ever! That would be
too grotesque. There's nothing more sublime than tears,
Nothing! —Shall I make them look ridiculous running
all the way down along this nose of mine?

LE BRET: Love's no more than chance! I saw Roxane,
watching your duel—her hand at her breast. Speak to
her man! Speak!

CYRANO: I can't. She might laugh at me; that is the one
thing in this world I fear!

(MARGUERITE *enters the box, addressing* CYRANO.)

MARGUERITE: Sir...

CYRANO: My God! Her Guardian.

MARGUERITE: A message for you; from your cousin.
She desires to know when and where she may see you
privately.

CYRANO: See me?

MARGUERITE: To see you. She has certain things to tell
you.

CYRANO: Certain—

MARGUERITE: Things.

CYRANO: (*To* LE BRET) My God!...

MARGUERITE: Where can you meet and talk a little?

CYRANO: Where?—I—Ah, my God!...my God!...

MARGUERITE: Well?

CYRANO: Yes! I am thinking.

MARGUERITE: And what do you think?

CYRANO: I...

LE BRET: Ragueneau's shop...

CYRANO: Yes! (*To* MARGUERITE) Ragueneau's shop. Ragueneau, the pastry cook.

MARGUERITE: We are agreed. Tomorrow, seven a.m. Until then—

CYRANO: I'll be there.

(MARGUERITE *goes out.*)

CYRANO: Le Bret! Me to see me!

LE BRET: You are not quite so gloomy.

CYRANO: After all, she knows that I exist—it doesn't matter why!

LE BRET: So now, you are going to be happy.

CYRANO: Now!... (*Beside himself*) I—I am going to be a storm—a flame—I need to fight whole armies all alone; I have ten hearts; I have a hundred arms; I feel too strong to war with mortals—Bring me giants!

(LISE, *who for some time has not been able to take her eyes off* CYRANO, *cannot help herself—she applauds and laughs.* CYRANO *does not take notice.* RAGUENEAU *enters, drunk.*)

RAGUENEAU: Cyrano!

LE BRET: Ragueneau!

CYRANO: What is it? Ragueneau—what's wrong with you?

RAGUENEAU: I need you! I can't go back to my shop!

CYRANO: Why not?

RAGUENEAU: Hundred against one—that's me—I'm the one—all because of a little song I wrote—hundred men, waiting, understand? The Great Bridge—way home—might be dangerous—would you permit me to spend the night with you?

CYRANO: A hundred men—is that all? You are going home! I'll be the man tonight that sees you home. Forward march!

(He pushes RAGUENEAU off.)

CYRANO: You follow—I want an audience!

LE BRET: A hundred against one—

CYRANO: Those are the odds tonight!

LE BRET: You cannot win—

CYRANO: There you go again, growling!

LE BRET: But why—?

CYRANO: Why...because if Ragueneau dies tonight, his shop will be closed tomorrow morning at seven.

(Sends LE BRET off—then follows. LISE looks on. She picks up the white rose CYRANO left and takes us into:)

Scene Two

(A bakery shop)

(Music continues as LISE walks through the bakery and exits. RAGUENEAU is discovered writing poetry.)

RAGUENEAU: Over the coppers of my kitchen
Flows the frosted-silver dawn.
Silence awhile the God
Who sings within thee, Ragueneau!

Lay down the lute,
The oven calls for thee!

(LISE *comes to him carrying a pile of paper bags she has brought from the kitchen.*)

RAGUENEAU: Paper bags? Thank you...God! My manuscripts! My sacred verses—butchered to make base packages of pastry! What a way to use poetry!

(CYRANO *enters hurriedly, a handkerchief tied around one hand.*)

CYRANO: What time is it? No, never mind. (*To* LISE) Would you bring me a pen and paper? (*To* RAGUENEAU) I expect someone, keep watch. Leave us here alone, when the time comes.

(RAGUENEAU *goes to the door of the shop.* LISE *brings the pen and paper to him, exits again.*)

CYRANO: Thank you. (*He sits.*) Only to write—to fold—to give it to her—and to go... (*Throws down the pen*) Coward. Yes. Why can't I just speak to her? Just one little word of all the many thousands I have here! (*Takes up the pen*) I'll write the letter I have written on my heart, torn up, and written over many times—so many times...that all I have to do is to remember, and to write it down.

(*He writes.* LISE *comes in. She puts a glass of water and a small plate of macaroons next to him, lingers behind him.*)

CYRANO: "Your eyes...Your lips...Looking at you, I grow faint with fear, Your friend—who loves you..." So. No signature; I'll give it to her myself.

(ROXANE *and* MARGUERITE *appear.*)

RAGUENEAU: Psst!—

(ROXANE *and* MARGUERITE *enter the shop.* RAGUENEAU *nods to* LISE, *who lingers. He exits.*)

CYRANO: She's here! *(He quickly puts the letter in his pocket. To* ROXANE*)* Welcome! *(To* MARGUERITE*)* Pardon me—one word—

MARGUERITE: Take two.

CYRANO: Have you a healthy appetite?

MARGUERITE: Wonderful!

CYRANO: Good. Do you like macaroons?

MARGUERITE: Always.

(He takes them from the table.)

CYRANO: Do you love Nature?

MARGUERITE: Mad about it.

CYRANO: Then go out and eat these in the street. Do not return—

MARGUERITE: Oh, but—

CYRANO: —until you finish them.

(As MARGUERITE *goes, he shoots a look to* LISE, *who leaves, eyeing* ROXANE.*)*

CYRANO: Blessed above all others be the hour when you remembered to remember me, and came to tell me...what?

ROXANE: First, let me thank you because...that man... that creature, whom your sword made sport of yesterday—his benefactor...

CYRANO: De Guiche?

ROXANE: Yes...he thinks himself in love with me and would force that man upon me—for a husband—

CYRANO: I understand—so much the better then! I fought, not for my nose but your bright eyes.... So...you came to tell me?

ROXANE: Before I can tell you.... Are you, I wonder, still the same big brother almost that you used to be when I was a child?

CYRANO: I remember every summer you came to Bergerac.

ROXANE: You used to make swords out of bulrushes!

CYRANO: And you—dandelion dolls with golden curls.

ROXANE: In those days, you did everything I wished.

CYRANO: Yes, I know, I remember.

ROXANE: Was I pretty?

CYRANO: Oh—not too plain!

(They laugh. She sees his hand—starts.)

ROXANE: What have you been doing to yourself? Let me see! Come sit over here.

CYRANO: Such a wise little mother.

(She unwraps the handkerchief from his hand, wets an end in the glass of water and begins to clean the blood away. A silence as he watches her.)

ROXANE: How did you do this?

CYRANO: Playing with some big boys by the Great Bridge.

ROXANE: Tell me, while I wash this blood away, how many you played with.

CYRANO: Oh, about a hundred.

ROXANE: Tell me.

CYRANO: No, you tell me what you were going to tell me—if you dare?

ROXANE: *(Still holding his hand)* I think I do dare now. Yes—I dare...Listen: I...love someone.

CYRANO: Ah!

ROXANE: Someone who does not know.

CYRANO: Ah!

ROXANE: At least—not yet.

CYRANO: Ah!

ROXANE: But he will know some day.

CYRANO: Ah!

ROXANE: Someone who loves me too and is afraid of me, and keeps away, and never says one word.

CYRANO: Ah!...

ROXANE: I know. I see him trying....

CYRANO: Ah!

ROXANE: There now! Is that better? *(She bandages the hand with her lace handkerchief, leaving his bloody one on the table.)* Besides—only to think—This is a secret. He is a soldier too. In your own regiment—

CYRANO: Ah!

ROXANE: Yes, in the Guards, your company too.

CYRANO: Ah!

ROXANE: And such a man!—He is proud—noble—strong—brave—beautiful—

CYRANO: Beautiful!—

ROXANE: What's the matter?

CYRANO: Nothing—just this—my sore hand!

ROXANE: Well, I love him. That is all.

CYRANO: You've never spoken?

ROXANE: Only our eyes...

CYRANO: You say he's in my company—in the guards?
His name?

ROXANE: Christian de Neuvillette.

CYRANO: Christian de Neuvillette? He is not in the
guards.

ROXANE: Yes. Since this morning.

CYRANO: So soon!...So soon we lose our hearts!—

MARGUERITE: *(Comes in)* I have eaten the macaroons.

CYRANO: Good! Now go out and read the wrapper!

(MARGUERITE exits.)

CYRANO: —But, Roxane! You, who love only words,
wit, the grand manner—Why, for all you know, the
man might be a fool.

ROXANE: Not with such eyes. I read his soul in them.

CYRANO: *(After a pause)* And you brought me here to
tell me this? I do not yet quite understand, Roxane,
the reason for your confidence.

ROXANE: They say that in your company—it frightens
me—you are all soldiers...I am so afraid for him!
And I thought you...you were so brave, so invincible
yesterday, against all those brutes!—If you, whom they
all fear—

CYRANO: I see. You want me to protect your little
soldier?

ROXANE: Will you? Just for me? Because I have always
been—your friend!

CYRANO: Of course...

ROXANE: Will you be his friend?

CYRANO: I will be his friend.

ROXANE: And never let him fight a duel?

CYRANO: No—never!

(She gives him a perfunctory kiss. LISE *enters to show* ROXANE *out.)*

ROXANE: Oh, but you are a darling!—I must go—You never told me about last night—Why, you must have been a hero! Have him write and tell me all about it—will you?

CYRANO: Of course...

ROXANE: I always did love you!—a hundred men against one—Well...goodbye. We are great friends, are we not?

CYRANO: Of course...

ROXANE: He must write to me—A hundred—You shall have to tell me the whole story some day, when I have time. A hundred men—what courage—

*(*LISE *and* ROXANE *regard each other for a moment.* ROXANE *goes.)*

CYRANO: Courage?...I have done better since!

*(*LISE *clears the table, taking* CYRANO'*s handkerchief with her, and exits as* CARBON *enters.)*

RAGUENEAU: You have another visitor.

CYRANO: *(Without moving)* Yes!

*(*CARBON, *captain of the guards, comes in with a drawn sword, along the whole blade of which is a collection of hats.)*

CARBON: Here he is!—Our hero!

CYRANO: *(Raises his head and salutes)* Captain!

CARBON: I was delayed by the crowd at the Great Bridge. Dead men everywhere. Look what I found in the street—dropped in their flight by the living. Our whole company is outside across the street. Come!

CYRANO: No—

CARBON: Come! They are waiting for you.

CYRANO: No! Please—

LE BRET: *(Enters)* The whole town's looking for you! Everyone knows—a triumph!

CYRANO: Why, yesterday I did not have so many friends!

LE BRET: Success at last! And Roxane?

CYRANO: Hush!...

RAGUENEAU: And another visitor.

(DE GUICHE appears, followed by VALVERT, whose arm is in a sling.)

CYRANO: Sir!—

DE GUICHE: I came to express my admiration. I have heard of your fight—

LE BRET: Bravo!

DE GUICHE: Your name is known already as a soldier. You're one of that wild regiment, aren't you?

CYRANO: The Guards, Yes.

CARBON: Cyrano!

CYRANO: This is our Captain.

CARBON: Sir.

DE GUICHE: *(A tiny bow to CARBON)* Poets are fashionable nowadays to have around. Would you care to join my following?

CYRANO: No, sir. I do not follow.

DE GUICHE: Your duel yesterday amused me. I might perhaps be in a position to help you. I suppose you've written a tragedy.

LE BRET: Now at last you will have it performed.

DE GUICHE: Yes. Why not? I am myself a dramatist. I may need to rewrite a few lines here and there.

CYRANO: Impossible. My blood curdles to think of altering one comma.

DE GUICHE: When I like a thing, I pay well.

CYRANO: Yes—but not so well as I—When I have written a line that sings itself so that I love the sound of it—I pay myself a hundred times.

DE GUICHE: Ah, you're proud.

CYRANO: Ah, you've noticed that?

CARBON: Whoever hired those men, he must be an angry man today.

RAGUENEAU: Who was it? Do you know?

DE GUICHE: I hired them to do the sort of work I don't soil my hands with—punishing a drunken poet...

(CYRANO *takes the sword with hats from* CARBON.)

CYRANO: Well sir, will you then be so good as to return these to your friends?

(*In a gesture of salute he causes all the hats to slide off at* DE GUICHE's *feet. A pause...*)

DE GUICHE: Have you read *Don Quixote*?

CYRANO: Yes, I have—and found myself the hero.

DE GUICHE: Read once more the chapter of the windmills.

CYRANO: Chapter thirteen.

DE GUICHE: Windmills, remember, if you fight with them—may swing round their huge arms and cast you down into the mire.

CYRANO: Or up—among the stars!

RAGUENEAU: I'll see you out, sir. The streets are not safe
these days.

(DE GUICHE *exits.* CARBON *makes kissing noises as*
VALVERT *follows* DE GUICHE. CARBON *and* RAGUENEAU
quickly gather up the hats and follow him out.)

LE BRET: You've done it now—you've made your
fortune!

CYRANO: There you go again, growling!—

LE BRET: This latest pose of yours—ruining every
chance that comes your way—becomes exaggerated—

CYRANO: Very well, then I exaggerate!

LE BRET: Oh, you do!

CYRANO: Yes I do; on principle. There are things in this
world a man does well to carry to extremes.

LE BRET: Stop trying to be Three Musketeers in one!
Fortune and glory.

CYRANO: What would you have me do? Seek for the
patronage of some great man and like a creeping vine
on a tall tree crawl upward, where I cannot stand
alone? No thank you! Dedicate, as others do, poems to
pawnbrokers? Be a buffoon in the vile hope of teasing
out a smile on some cold face? No thank you! Eat a
lump for breakfast every morning? Make my knees
callous, and cultivate a supple spine—wear out my
belly groveling in the dust? No thank you! Use the fire
God gave me to burn incense all day long? No thank
you. Shall I go leaping into ladies' laps and lick their
fingers? No thank you. Publish verses at my own
expense? No thank you. Be the patron saint of a
small group of literary souls who dine together every
Tuesday? No, I thank you! Shall I labor night and
day to build a reputation on one song and never write
another? No thank you! Calculate, scheme, be afraid.

Love more to make a visit than a poem. Seek
introductions, favors, influences?—No thank you! No,
I thank you, and again I thank you! *(Pause)* But...to sing,
to laugh, to dream. To walk in my own way and be
alone, free, with an eye to see things as they are, a voice
that means manhood—to cock my hat where I choose.
At a word. A yes, a no. To fight...to write. To travel any
road under the sun, under the stars. Never to write a
line I have not heard in my own heart; yet, with all
modesty to say: "My soul be satisfied with flowers,
with fruit, with weeds even; but gather them in the one
garden you may call your own." So, when I win some
triumph, by some chance, render no share to Caesar—
in a word, I am too proud to be a parasite, and if my
nature wants the germ that grows towering to heaven
like the mountain pine—I stand, not high it may
be—but alone!

LE BRET: Alone, yes! But why stand against the world?
What devil has possessed you now, to go everywhere
making yourself enemies?

CYRANO: Watching you other people making friends
everywhere—as a dog makes friends! I mark the
manner of these canine courtesies and think, "My
friends are of a cleaner breed. Here comes—thank God!
—another enemy!" It is my pleasure to displease. I love
hatred!

(LE BRET goes to CYRANO.)

LE BRET: Yes...tell this to all the world—and then to me
say very softly that...she loves you not.

CYRANO: Quiet!

(RAGUENEAU enters with CARBON and CHRISTIAN.)

RAGUENEAU: "Then as I end the refrain...thrust home!"
"As I end the refrain thrust home!" God...what a line.
(He calls to LISE.) Lise, some wine, quick! To celebrate!

I'm alive today because of you, my friend, and Cyrano. I'll write no more songs. Better a fat pastry cook than a dead poet.

(LISE *enters and puts tray down on table.*)

RAGUENEAU: Cyrano!—the story of last night.

CYRANO: *(Who has moved away, not seeing* CHRISTIAN*)* In a moment...

RAGUENEAU: The story of the combat! An example for—this young tadpole here.

CHRISTIAN: Tadpole?

RAGUENEAU: Yes, you!—Christian: You should know there is a certain subject—I would say, a certain object—never to be mentioned among us: utterly unmentionable!

CHRISTIAN: And that is?

RAGUENEAU: Look at us!

(RAGUENEAU *and* CARBON *mime large imaginary noses with their fingers.*)

RAGUENEAU: You understand?

CHRISTIAN: Why, yes; the nose.

CARBON & RAGUENEAU: Sh!

CARBON: We never speak that word. To breathe it is to have to do with him.

RAGUENEAU: Would you die before your time?

CARBON: Just mention anything convex...or cartilaginous...one word— one syllable—one gesture— one sneeze—your handkerchief becomes your shroud!

CHRISTIAN: *(To* LE BRET*)* Sir, what is the proper thing to do when a Guardsman grows too boastful?

LE BRET: Prove to him that one may be a recruit and have courage.

CHRISTIAN: I thank you.

(CYRANO *is heading for the door.*)

RAGUENEAU: Cyrano, the story!

CARBON: Come—yes, the story!

CYRANO: Oh yes. My story! Well... I marched on, all alone to meet those devils. Overhead the moon hung like a gold watch at the fob of heaven, 'til suddenly some angel rubbed a cloud, as it might be his handkerchief, across the shining crystal, and— the night came down. No lamps in those back streets— it was so dark! You could not see beyond—

CHRISTIAN: Your nose.

(*Silence. Pause.* CYRANO *turns to look.*)

CYRANO: Who is that man there?

CARBON: A recruit—arrived this morning.

CYRANO: A recruit—

CARBON: His name is Christian de Neuvillette.

CYRANO: (*Controls himself*) Oh...I—I see. Very well, as I was saying—It grew dark, you could not see your hand in front of your eyes. I marched on, thinking how, all for the sake of this old drunk who writes a bawdy song whenever he takes—

CHRISTIAN: A nose-full—

CYRANO: —takes a notion, whenever he takes a notion—For his sake, I might antagonize some dangerous man, one powerful enough to make me pay—

CHRISTIAN: Through the nose—

CYRANO: —pay the Piper. After all, I thought, why am I
putting in my—

CHRISTIAN: Nose—

CYRANO: —my oar...why am I putting in my oar?
The quarrel's none of mine. However—now I am—
here, I may as well go through with it. Suddenly,
a sword flashed in the dark. I caught it fair—

CHRISTIAN: On the nose—

CYRANO: On my blade. Before I knew it, there I was—

CHRISTIAN: Rubbing noses—

CYRANO: Crossing swords with half a dozen at once.
I handed one—

CHRISTIAN: A nosegay—

CYRANO: He went down; the rest gave way; I charged—

CHRISTIAN: Nose in the air—

CYRANO: I skewered two of them—disarmed a third—
paf! And I countered—

CHRISTIAN: Pif!

CYRANO: Everybody out!

CARBON: At last—the old lion wakes!

CYRANO: Leave me here alone with that man!

CARBON: Come! It frightens me to think what will
happen.

LE BRET: He'll have that man chopped into sausage.

RAGUENEAU: Mince meat. One of my pies. Am I pale?

LE BRET: White as a fresh napkin.

(They all go.)

CYRANO: To my arms!

CHRISTIAN: Sir? ...

CYRANO: You have courage!

CHRISTIAN: Oh, that!

CYRANO: You are brave—that pleases me.

CHRISTIAN: You're not angry?

CYRANO: Do you not know I am her brother? Come!

CHRISTIAN: Whose?—

CYRANO: Hers—Roxane!

CHRISTIAN: You? Her...brother?

CYRANO: Her cousin. Much the same thing.

CHRISTIAN: And she has told you?...

CYRANO: Everything.

CHRISTIAN: She loves me?

CYRANO: Perhaps.

CHRISTIAN: Oh, God!—More than I can say, I'm honored— *(Takes both of his hands)*

CYRANO: This is rather sudden.

CHRISTIAN: Please forgive me—

CYRANO: You are a handsome devil!

CHRISTIAN: On my honor—if you knew how much I have admired—

CYRANO: Yes, oh really, yes?—and all those noses.

CHRISTIAN: Please! I apologize.

CYRANO: Accepted. Roxane expects a letter—

CHRISTIAN: Not from me?—

CYRANO: Yes. Why not?

CHRISTIAN: No—once I write, it ruins everything!

CYRANO: Why?

CHRISTIAN: Because...because I'm a fool! Stupid enough to hang myself.

CYRANO: You are not a fool. I wish you were. You did not attack me like a fool.

CHRISTIAN: Anyone can pick a quarrel. Yes, I have a sort of rough and ready soldier's tongue, I know that. But with any woman—paralyzed, speechless, dumb. I can only look at them. Sometimes, when I go away...their eyes—

CYRANO: Stay! You'll see their hearts.

CHRISTIAN: No, I am one of those—I know—those men who never can make love.

CYRANO: Strange...Now it seems I, if I put my mind to it, I might perhaps make love well.

CHRISTIAN: Oh, if I had words to say what I have here!

CYRANO: If only I could be a handsome little soldier boy with eyes!—

CHRISTIAN: Besides, you know Roxane—how sensitive. One rough word and the sweet illusion—gone.

CYRANO: I wish you might be my interpreter.

CHRISTIAN: I wish I had your wit—

(A pause)

CYRANO: Borrow it, then!

CHRISTIAN: What?

CYRANO: Your beautiful young manhood—lend me that, and we two make one hero of romance! Would you dare repeat to her the words I gave you, day by day?

CHRISTIAN: What do you mean?

CYRANO: I mean Roxane shall have no disillusionment! Come, shall we win her both together? Take the soul within this body of mine and breathe it into you? So—there's my heart with your heart now!

CHRISTIAN: But—Cyrano!—

CYRANO: But—Christian, why not?

CHRISTIAN: I am afraid—

CYRANO: I know. Afraid that when you have her all alone, you lose all. Have no fear. It is yourself she loves. Give her yourself put into words—my words, upon your lips. Will you, will you?

CHRISTIAN: Does it mean so much to you?

CYRANO: Yes, it does, it means—a comedy, a situation for a poet! Come—let's collaborate? I'll be your cloak of darkness, your enchanted sword, your ring to charm the fairy princess!

CHRISTIAN: But the letter—I cannot write—

CYRANO: Oh yes, the letter. (*He takes from his pocket the letter that he has written.*) Here.

CHRISTIAN: What is this?

CYRANO: All there; all but the address.

CHRISTIAN: I—

CYRANO: Oh, you may send it. It will do.

CHRISTIAN: But why have you done this?

CYRANO: I have amused myself, as we all do, we poets—writing vows. Take it. Bring my fantasies to life—I have loosed these loves like doves into the air. Give them a home—Take it!

CHRISTIAN: First, there must be a few changes here and there. Written at random, can it fit Roxane?

CYRANO: Like her own glove.

CHRISTIAN: No, but—

CYRANO: Christian, have faith—faith in the love of women for themselves—Roxane will know this letter for her own!

CHRISTIAN: My friend!

(CHRISTIAN *throws himself into the arms of* CYRANO. *They stand embraced.* LE BRET, RAGUENEAU, *and* CARBON *appear.* LISE *as well, from the kitchen)*

CARBON: Well, well, well!

RAGUENEAU: Here's our devil...Christianized!

LE BRET: Yes! Offend one nostril and he turns the other.

CHRISTIAN: See! Now we're allowed to talk about his nose.

CYRANO: (*Grabbing* CHRISTIAN's *nose and holding tight*) Oh no we're not. Out! Out! All of you. Out! Out!

(LISE *collects the wine glasses.* CYRANO *does not notice her. She leaves. He pushes the others towards the exit. Standing alone, he turns back into the room and slowly unwinds* ROXANE's *lace handkerchief from his hand, brings it to his eyes, and finally weeps. The lights begin to change, music up, taking us to....)*

(*End of Scene Two*)

Scene Three

(*A garden*)

(*Music out.* MARGUERITE *enters, calling up to a balcony window.)*

MARGUERITE: Roxane! Are you ready? We are late!

ROXANE: *(From within)* One moment, I'll be there in just
a moment.

MARGUERITE: Hurry, dear—we shall miss the tender
passion!

(RAGUENEAU is heard singing offstage right.)

MARGUERITE: A serenade. How pleasant.

(RAGUENEAU enters singing.)

RAGUENEAU: *(Sings)* "I who praise your lillies fair,
But long to love your roses...

CYRANO: *(Entering)* No, no, no, F natural, you
natural-born fool.

MARGUERITE: Did you train this virtuoso?

CYRANO: No, I did not. *(To RAGUENEAU)* Go away now,
Ragueneau, you're drunk. Go and sing that song to
Montfleury—and tell him I sent you. Sing it out of tune.

(RAGUENEAU exits.)

ROXANE: *(From offstage)* Is that you? Cyrano!

CYRANO: Yes it is.

ROXANE: I'll be out—wait—

CYRANO: *(To MARGUERITE)* You are leaving?

MARGUERITE: Our neighbor across the way receives on
Thursday nights—we are to have a psycho-colloquy
upon the tender passion.

CYRANO: Ah—the tender—

MARGUERITE: Passion.

CYRANO: I see.

MARGUERITE: Roxane! We haven't much time.

(ROXANE enters, holding a large bunch of letters.)

CYRANO: I came here as usual, as I do, week upon week, to inquire after Christian—our friend with the great soul.

ROXANE: He is beautiful and brilliant—and I love him! No man ever so beautifully said those things—those pretty nothings that are everything—

CYRANO: Really?

ROXANE: Oh, men! You think a man who has a handsome face must be a fool.

CYRANO: He talks well about...matters of the heart?

ROXANE: He does not talk—he rhapsodizes.

CYRANO: He...writes well?

ROXANE: Wonderfully. Listen now: *(Reads)* "Take my heart; I shall have it all the more. Plucking the flowers, we keep the plant in bloom—" Well?

CYRANO: Pooh!

ROXANE: And this: "Knowing you have in store more heart to give than I to find heart room —"

CYRANO: First he has too much heart, then too little. Just how much heart does he need?

ROXANE: You are teasing me—you are jealous.

CYRANO: Jealous?

ROXANE: Yes, of his poetry—you poets are like that...and these last lines:
"Sending you kisses through my fingertips—
Lady, oh read my letter with your lips!"

CYRANO: Ah, yes, those last lines...but he overwrites!

ROXANE: Listen to this...

CYRANO: You know them all by heart?

ROXANE: Every one.

CYRANO: I may call that flattering.

ROXANE: He is a master.

CYRANO: Oh—come!

ROXANE: Yes—a master!

CYRANO: A master—if you will!

MARGUERITE: Sir, De Guiche is coming! (*To* CYRANO, *pushing him toward the house.*) Go inside—if he sees you here he may suspect—

ROXANE: —My secret! Yes; he is in love with me and he is powerful. I don't want him to know.

CYRANO: (*Going into house*) All right! All right!

DE GUICHE: Good evening.

ROXANE: (*To* DE GUICHE, *as he enters*) We were just going—

DE GUICHE: I came to say goodbye.

ROXANE: You are leaving?

DE GUICHE: Yes—for the front.

ROXANE: Ah!

DE GUICHE: And tonight!

ROXANE: Ah!

DE GUICHE: My departure leaves you...cold?

ROXANE: Oh! Not that.

DE GUICHE: It has left me desolate—When shall I see you again? Ever? Did you know I was made colonel?

ROXANE: Bravo.

DE GUICHE: Regiment of the Guards.

ROXANE: Of the Guards?—

DE GUICHE: Cyrano's regiment. Your cousin, the mighty man of words! Perhaps there we may have an accounting.

ROXANE: Are you sure the Guards are ordered?

DE GUICHE: Under my command! What is it?

ROXANE: To the war—perhaps never again to— When a woman cares, is that nothing?

DE GUICHE: You say this now—to me—now, this very moment?

ROXANE: Tell me something: Cyrano—what will you do to him? Order him into danger? He loves that! I know what I should do.

DE GUICHE: What?

ROXANE: Leave him here with his soldiers to sit all through the war. That would torture him—I know his nature.

DE GUICHE: Oh! Women! Who but a woman would have thought of this?

ROXANE: You'll have your revenge!

DE GUICHE: —You play your little games, do you?

ROXANE: Sometimes...

DE GUICHE: I am mad about you!—Listen—I leave tonight—but—let you through my hands now, when I feel you trembling? Close by, the priests have their convent. I'll wait there. Later I'll come to you masked, after everyone has gone to sleep. *(Kisses her hand)* Will that content you?

ROXANE: Yes—my friend!

(He goes out.)

MARGUERITE: *(Imitating* ROXANE*)* Yes—my friend!

ROXANE: Not a word to Cyrano—he would never forgive me if he knew I stole his war! *(She calls toward the house)* Cousin!

(CYRANO comes in.)

ROXANE: If Christian comes, tell him to wait.

CYRANO: When he does come, what will you talk about? You always know beforehand.

ROXANE: You will not tell him, will you?

CYRANO: I am dumb.

ROXANE: About nothing! Or about everything—I will say: "Speak of love in your own words—Improvise! Rhapsodize! Be eloquent!"

CYRANO: Good!

ROXANE: Sh!—

CYRANO: Sh!—

ROXANE: Not a word!

CYRANO: *(Bowing)* Thank you so much.

ROXANE: He must be unprepared.

(She exits with MARGUERITE.)

CYRANO: Of course. *(Calls)* Christian!

(CHRISTIAN enters.)

CYRANO: I have tonight's theme—Here's your chance to surpass yourself, no time to lose—Come! Look intelligent—Come home and learn your lines.

CHRISTIAN: No.

CYRANO: What?

CHRISTIAN: I'll wait here for Roxane—

CYRANO: What lunacy is this? Come quickly!

CHRISTIAN: No, I've had enough—taking my words, my letters, all from you—making our love a little comedy! It was a game at first; but now—she cares...thanks to you. I am not afraid. I'll speak for myself now.

CYRANO: Undoubtedly!

CHRISTIAN: I will. You were right. I am no fool. By God, I know enough to take a woman in my arms!

(ROXANE *appears.*)

CHRISTIAN: There she is now...

(CYRANO *makes to leave.*)

CHRISTIAN: Cyrano, wait! Stay here!

CYRANO: Speak for yourself, my friend! (*He goes out.*)

ROXANE: Is that you, Christian? Let us stay here, in the twilight. The air is so lovely. We can be alone. Sit down there.

(*They sit on the bench.*)

ROXANE: Now tell me things.

CHRISTIAN: (*After a silence*) I love you!

ROXANE: (*Closes her eyes*) Yes, speak to me about love...

CHRISTIAN: I love you.

ROXANE: Now be eloquent!...

CHRISTIAN: I love—

ROXANE: (*Opens her eyes*) Improvise! Rhapsodize!

CHRISTIAN: I love you...so!

ROXANE: Of course. And then?...

CHRISTIAN: And then...Oh, I should be so happy if you loved me too! Roxane, say that you love me too!

ROXANE: I asked for cream! You give me milk and water. Tell me first, a little, how you love me.

CHRISTIAN: Very much.

ROXANE: Oh—tell me how you feel!

CHRISTIAN: Your throat...if only I might...kiss it—

ROXANE: Christian!

CHRISTIAN: I love you so!

ROXANE: Again?

CHRISTIAN: No, not again—I do not love you—

ROXANE: That is better....

CHRISTIAN: I adore you!

ROXANE: Oh!—

CHRISTIAN: I know; I grow absurd.

ROXANE: And that displeases me as much as if you had grown ugly.

CHRISTIAN: I—I love—

ROXANE: I know; you love me. Goodnight! *(She goes to the house.)*

CHRISTIAN: No, but wait—please—let me—I was going to say—

ROXANE: That you adore me. Yes; I know that too. No!...Go away!

CHRISTIAN: I...I...

CYRANO: *(Enters)* A great success!

CHRISTIAN: Help me!

CYRANO: Not I.

CHRISTIAN: I cannot live unless she loves me—now, this moment!

CYRANO: How the devil am I to teach you now—this moment?

CHRISTIAN: I shall die!—

CYRANO: Less noise!

CHRISTIAN: Oh, I—

CYRANO: It does seem fairly dark—

CHRISTIAN: *(Excitedly)* Well?—Well?—Well?

CYRANO: Let's see what we can do; it's more than you deserve—Stand over there. Idiot —there! —before the balcony—let me stand underneath. I'll whisper to you what to say.

CHRISTIAN: She may hear—she may—

CYRANO: Less noise! Call her!

CHRISTIAN: Roxane!

ROXANE: *(Coming onto the balcony)* Who is calling?

CHRISTIAN: I—

ROXANE: Who?

CHRISTIAN: Christian.

ROXANE: You again?

CHRISTIAN: I had to tell you—I only wanted to say....

CYRANO: *(Under the balcony)* Good—keep your voice down.

ROXANE: No. Go away. You do not love me anymore!

CHRISTIAN: *(To whom* CYRANO *whispers his words.)* No—no—not any more—I love you...evermore... and ever...more and more!

ROXANE: A little better...

CHRISTIAN: *(Same business)* Love grows and struggles like...an angry child...breaking my heart...his cradle....

ROXANE: *(Coming out on the balcony.)* Better still—
But...such a babe is dangerous; why not have
smothered it newborn?

CHRISTIAN: *(Same business)* And so I do...And yet he
lives...I found...as you shall find this newborn babe...
an infant...Hercules!

ROXANE: Good! But tell me now why you speak so
haltingly—has your imagination gone lame?

CYRANO: *(Puts* CHRISTIAN *under the balcony and stands in
his place)* Here—this is getting too difficult!

ROXANE: Your words tonight hesitate. Why?

CYRANO: *(In a low voice, imitating* CHRISTIAN*)* Through
the warm summer gloom they grope in darkness
toward the light of you.

ROXANE: My words, well aimed, find you—more
readily.

CYRANO: My heart is open wide and waits for them—
too large a mark to miss! Moreover—your words fall to
me swiftly. Mine more slowly rise.

ROXANE: Yet not so slowly as they did at first.

CYRANO: They have learned the way, and you have
welcomed them.

ROXANE: *(Softly)* Am I so far above you now?

CYRANO: So far—if you let fall upon me one hard word,
out of that height—you crush me!

ROXANE: I'll come down—

CYRANO: No!

ROXANE: Stand on the bench. Come nearer!

CYRANO: *(Recoils into the shadow)* No!—

ROXANE: And why—so great a "No"?

CYRANO: Let me enjoy the one moment I ever—my one chance to speak to you...unseen!

ROXANE: Unseen?

CYRANO: Yes!...yes...Night makes all things dimly beautiful. There's one veil over us both—you see only the dark figure of a man standing in the gloom, and I, the whiteness of a summer gown—you are all light— I am all shadow!... How can you know what this moment means to me? If I was ever eloquent....

ROXANE: You were eloquent.

CYRANO: You have not heard 'til now my own heart speaking.

ROXANE: Why not?

CYRANO: Until now I spoke through that sweet drunkenness you pour into the world out of your eyes! Oh, but tonight...tonight my own heart speaks for the first time!

ROXANE: For the first time—Your voice, even, is not the same.

CYRANO: How should it be? I have another voice—my own, myself, daring—where was I?...I forget!...Forgive me. This is all sweet like a dream...strange—like a dream.

ROXANE: How, strange?

CYRANO: Is it not so to be myself to you and have no fear of moving you to laughter?

ROXANE: Laughter—why?

CYRANO: Because... What am I... What is any man, that he dare to ask for you? Therefore, my heart hides behind phrases. I make rhymes for you.

ROXANE: Yes...poetry.

CYRANO: No poetry. Not now. Shall we insult nature, this night, this moment, shall we set all this to phrases? Love hates that game of words! It is a crime to fence with life! I tell you, there comes one moment, once— and God help those who pass that moment by— when Beauty stands looking into the soul with grave, sweet eyes that sicken at pretty words!

ROXANE: And when that moment comes to you and me—what words will you?...

CYRANO: All those, all those, all those that blossom in my heart, I'll fling to you—armfuls of loose bloom! Love, I love beyond breath, beyond reason, beyond love's own power of loving! Your name is like a golden bell hung in my heart, and when I think of you I tremble, and the bell swings and rings—"Roxane!"... Roxane!...along my veins, "Roxane!...I know all small forgotten things that once meant you—I remember last year, the First of May, a little before noon, you had your hair drawn low, that one time only. Is that strange? You know how after looking at the sun, one sees red suns everywhere? So, for hours after the flood of sunshine that you are, my eyes are blinded by your burning hair!

ROXANE: Yes...that is...love—

CYRANO: Yes, that is Love—that wind of terrible and jealous beauty, blowing over me—that dark fire, that music...Yet Love seeketh not his own...Darling, you may take my happiness to make you happier, even though you never know I gave it to you—only let me hear sometimes, all alone, the distant laughter of your joy!... I never look at you, but there's some new virtue born in me, some new courage. Do you begin to understand, a little? Can you feel my soul, there in the darkness, breathe on you?—Oh, but tonight, now, I dare say these things—I...to you...and you hear them!...It is too much! In my most sweet—unreasonable dreams, I have not hoped for this! Now let me

die—having lived. It is my voice, mine, my own that
makes you tremble there in the green gloom above
me—for you do tremble, as a blossom among the
leaves—you tremble, and I can feel, all the way down
along these jasmine branches, whether you will or no,
the passion of you trembling...

ROXANE: Yes, I do tremble...and I weep...and I love
you...and I am yours...and you have made me thus!

CYRANO: I have done this, to you—I, myself... Only...

CHRISTIAN: *(Under the balcony)* Let me ask one thing
more—one kiss.

CYRANO: You!

ROXANE: One? You ask me for—

CYRANO: I... Yes, but—I mean— *(To* CHRISTIAN*)* You go
too far!

CHRISTIAN: She is willing!—Why not make the most of
it?

CYRANO: *(To* ROXANE*)* I did ask...but I know I ask too
much....

ROXANE: Only one—is that all?

CYRANO: I know—I frighten you—I ask...I ask you to
refuse—

CHRISTIAN: *(To* CYRANO*)* But why? Why? Why?

CYRANO: Christian, be quiet!

ROXANE: What is that you say to yourself?

CYRANO: I am angry with myself because I go too far,
and so I say to myself: "Christian, be quiet!"

CHRISTIAN: Win me that kiss!

CYRANO: No.

CHRISTIAN: Sooner or later...

CYRANO: True...that is true.... Sooner or later, it will be so because you are young and she is beautiful—since it must be, I had rather be myself—the cause of what must be.

ROXANE: Are you still there? We were speaking of—

CYRANO: A kiss. The word is sweet—What will the deed be? Are your lips afraid? Not much afraid— not too much!

ROXANE: Hush—come...

CYRANO: (*To* CHRISTIAN) Go on!—Climb!—

CHRISTIAN: (*Hesitates*) No—would you?—not yet—

CYRANO: (*Pushing him*) Climb up, animal!

(CHRISTIAN *climbs onto the balcony.*)

CHRISTIAN: Roxane!... (*He takes her in his arms and kisses her.*)

CYRANO: (*Very low*) Ah!...Roxane!... I have won what I have won—the feast of love, and I am faint with hunger! Yet...I have something here that is mine now— and was not mine before I spoke the words that won her—not for me.... She's kissing my words, my words, upon his lips! (*A pause*) Someone is there. A priest. (*He pretends to be running, as if he has arrived from a distance, then calls up to the balcony.*) Hello!

ROXANE: Who is it?

CYRANO: I. Is Christian there with you?

CHRISTIAN: Cyrano!

ROXANE: Cyrano.

CYRANO: Hello!

ROXANE: I am coming down.

(They disappear into the house. The PRIEST *enters, carrying a lantern.)*

CYRANO: Good evening, Father. May I help you?

PRIEST: *(To* CYRANO*)* I am looking for the house of Roxane Robin!

CYRANO: You have found it. What is it?

PRIEST: A letter. A very distinguished gentleman gave it to me!

CYRANO: Oh, I see. She will be here presently.

*(*ROXANE *and* CHRISTIAN *come in, followed by* MARGUERITE*.)*

CYRANO: A letter for you, Roxane.

ROXANE: *(To* CYRANO*)* De Guiche!

CYRANO: Father, may I have a word? *(He pulls the* PRIEST *away.)*

CHRISTIAN: He dares—

ROXANE: It will not be for long when he learns that I love you. *(She reads the letter to herself.)* "Roxane, the drums are beating, and the regiment arms for the march. I shall be with you soon. I send this first by a young monk, who understands nothing of this. Be alone tonight. Send away your guardian..."— et cetera. *(To the* PRIEST*)* Father, this letter concerns you... *(To* CHRISTIAN*)* —and you. Listen: *(She pretends to read from the letter aloud.)* "Roxane: The Church will have its way, although against your will; that is why I am sending this to you by way of this young priest, intelligent, discreet. You will communicate to him our order to perform, here and at once, the rite of...Holy Matrimony. You and Christian will be married privately in your house. I have sent him to you. I know you hesitate. Be resigned, nevertheless, to the Church's command.

PRIEST: A great gentleman! I said so.

ROXANE: *(To* CHRISTIAN*)* Am I a good reader of letters?

CHRISTIAN: Careful!

PRIEST: *(To* CYRANO*)* You are to be—

CHRISTIAN: I am to be the bridegroom!

PRIEST: Oh? Perhaps I should consult the monsignor—

ROXANE: *(Quickly)* "Postscript: Give to the convent in my name a generous sum of money.

PRIEST: *(A beat of silence. To* ROXANE*)* Resign yourself!

ROXANE: I am resigned.... *(To* CYRANO*)* De Guiche is coming. Keep him out here until we are wed.

CYRANO: I understand! *(To the* PRIEST*)* How long will you be, father?

PRIEST: Oh, less than a quarter of an hour. It takes no time to marry.

CYRANO: *(Hurrying them into the house.)* Hurry—I'll wait here—What to do?

(He takes MARGUERITE*'s shawl, throws it over his head. She goes.)*

CYRANO: Now, to delay De Guiche that quarter of an hour. *(He climbs up the side of the balcony.)*

CYRANO: I must arrive from on high. I must pitch my voice a bit higher as well.

DE GUICHE: *(Enters, masked, groping in the dark toward the house.)* Where is that priest? Here is the house— all dark—damn this mask!—

*(*CYRANO *leaps from the balcony,* DE GUICHE *leaps back.)*

DE GUICHE: Why...where did you fall—from?

CYRANO: *(Sits up and speaks with another voice)* The moon!

DE GUICHE: You—

CYRANO: From the moon, the moon! I fell out of the moon!

DE GUICHE: You must be mad—

CYRANO: Where am I?

DE GUICHE: Please let me pass.

CYRANO: Where am I? You can tell me. Tell the truth—I can take it.

DE GUICHE: Let me pass, I said!

CYRANO: Where have I been drawn by the dead weight of my posterior?

DE GUICHE: Sir. I repeat—

CYRANO: *(With a sudden cry)* His face! My God—black!

DE GUICHE: *(Carries his hand to his mask)* Oh!

CYRANO: Are you a native? Is this Africa?

DE GUICHE: —This mask!

CYRANO: Are we in Venice? Genoa?

DE GUICHE: A lady is waiting for me.

CYRANO: So, this is Paris!

(DE GUICHE *smiles, in spite of himself.)*

CYRANO: Ah! You smile?

DE GUICHE: I do. Now, kindly permit me—

CYRANO: *(Delighted)* Well, well!—Excuse my appearance. I arrive by the last thunderbolt—a trifle singed as I came through the ether. These long journeys—you know! There are so few conveniences! My eyes are full of stardust. On my spurs, some sort of fur...look—on my shoulder—That's a comet's hair! *(He blows something from the back of his hand.)*

DE GUICHE: *(Grows angry)* Sir—

CYRANO: Well—when I write my book and tell the tale of my adventures—all these little stars that shake out of my cloak—I must save those to use for asterisks!

DE GUICHE: That will do now. I wish to....

CYRANO: Yes, yes—I know—I read minds. You wish to know by what mysterious means I reached the moon?— Well—confidentially—it was a new invention of my own.

DE GUICHE: You're drunk—as well as mad!

CYRANO: I discovered not one scheme merely, but five—five ways to violate the virgin sky!

DE GUICHE: *(Interested now)* Five?

CYRANO: As, for instance—having stripped myself bare as a wax candle, adorn my form with crystal vials filled with morning dew, and so be drawn aloft, as the sun rises, drinking the mist of dawn!

DE GUICHE: *(Takes a step toward* CYRANO*)* Yes, that makes one.

CYRANO: Or, sealing up the air in a cedar chest, rarefy it by means of mirrors.

DE GUICHE: Two.

CYRANO: Again, I might construct a rocket, in the form of a huge locust, driven by impulses of invasive saltpeter from the rear, upward, by leaps and bounds!

DE GUICHE: Three.

CYRANO: Or, again, smoke having a natural tendency to rise, blow in a globe enough to raise me.

DE GUICHE: Four.

CYRANO: Finally—seated on an iron plate, I hurl a magnet in the air—the iron follows—I catch the

magnet—hurl again and so proceed indefinitely.
Hurl and rise! Hurl and rise!

DE GUICHE: Five!—all excellent—and which did you
choose?

CYRANO: Why, none of them...a sixth.

DE GUICHE: Which was?

CYRANO: Guess!

DE GUICHE: You're drunk; you're mad! But at least
you're interesting.

CYRANO: Have you guessed it yet?

DE GUICHE: Why, no.

CYRANO: The ocean! What hour its rising tide seeks the
full moon, I laid me on the strand, fresh from the spray,
my head fronting the moonbeams, since the hair retains
moisture and so I slowly rose as upon angels' wings,
effortlessly, upward—then suddenly I felt a shock!—
and then...

DE GUICHE: And then?

CYRANO: And then— (*In his own voice*) The time is
up!—You are now free; and—they are bound—
in wedlock. (*He throws off the shawl.*)

DE GUICHE: Am I drunk too? That voice...and that
nose!—Cyrano!

CYRANO: Cyrano! This very moment, they have
exchanged vows.

DE GUICHE: Who?

(ROXANE *and* CHRISTIAN *appear followed by the* PRIEST *and*
MARGUERITE.)

DE GUICHE: My sincere compliments! (*To* CYRANO) You
also, my inventor of machines! Your rigmarole would

have detained a saint entering paradise—decidedly you must not fail to write that book someday!

CYRANO: Sir, I engage myself to do so. May I present the handsome couple whom you—and God—have joined together!

DE GUICHE: Quite so. *(Turns to* ROXANE*)* Kindly bid your...husband goodbye!

ROXANE: What?

DE GUICHE: *(To* CHRISTIAN*)* Your regiment leaves tonight, sir. Report at once!

ROXANE: You mean for the front? The war?

DE GUICHE: Certainly!

ROXANE: I thought the Cadets were not going—

DE GUICHE: Oh yes, they are! Now!

ROXANE: Christian!

DE GUICHE: *(To* CYRANO*)* The bridal night is not so near! *(He goes.)*

CYRANO: Somehow that news fails to disquiet me.

CHRISTIAN: Kiss me...kiss me.

CYRANO: There...that will do now—Come! Away! Quickly, Christian.

(He sends CHRISTIAN *out. He gives the shawl to* MARGUERITE *and starts to go.* MARGUERITE *and the* PRIEST *hold* ROXANE.*)*

ROXANE: Take care of him for me—Promise never to let him do anything dangerous!

CYRANO: I'll do my best—I cannot promise—

ROXANE: Make him be careful!

CYRANO: Yes—I'll try—

ROXANE: Be sure to keep him dry and warm!

CYRANO: Yes, yes—if possible—

ROXANE: See that he remains faithful!—

CYRANO: Of course! If—

ROXANE: And have him write to me every single day!

CYRANO: *(Stops)* That, I promise you!

(Music up)

(Curtain)

END OF ACT ONE

ACT TWO

Scene One

(A camp)

(A battlefield camp—cold and gray. It is just daylight. CHRISTIAN *by a fire asleep. Wind.* CYRANO *enters.)*

CARBON: Halt, who goes there?

CYRANO: Bergerac! Who else?

LE BRET: Thank God again.

CYRANO: *(Trying not to wake* CHRISTIAN*)* Hush.

LE BRET: Wounded?

CYRANO: No—they always miss me—quite a habit by this time.

LE BRET: Yes—go right on—risk your life every morning before breakfast to send a letter!

CYRANO: I promised he'd write every single day....
(Looks over at him) The boy looks pale when he's asleep—thin, too—starving to death. Handsome, nonetheless...

LE BRET: You get some sleep!

CYRANO: Now, now—you old bear, no growling!—I am careful—you know I am—Every night when I cross the enemy lines I wait until they're drunk.

LE BRET: Fine war—fine situation. Yes, you can laugh—risking a life like yours to carry letters.

CYRANO: You up there. Why the long face?

SOLDIER: I have something on my mind that troubles me.

CYRANO: What is that?

SOLDIER: My stomach.

CYRANO: So have I.

LE BRET: No doubt you enjoy this.

CYRANO: It keeps me looking young.

SOLDIER: My teeth are growing rusty.

CYRANO: Sharpen them.

LE BRET: Always the clever answer.

CYRANO: Always the answer—yes! Let me die so, under some rosy-colored sunset—saying a good thing for a good cause! Let me fall by the sword, the point of honor—by one worthy enough to be my opponent —steel in my heart and laughter on my lips!

LE BRET: All very well—we are hungry!

SOLDIER: I have no stomach for this war—may as well die.

(*Scripted ad-libs and general grumbling*)

SOLDIER #2: Yes, I'm starving.

SOLDIER #3: Hungry like a wolf.

CARBON: Cyrano, listen to these men.

CYRANO: You think of nothing but yourselves. You up there, you were a shepherd once—your pipe now! Play to these belly-worshippers. A small, sad, demure tune whose every note is like a little sister. Play.

(The pipe begins.)

CYRANO: Now, dream, while over the stops your fingers dance. Recall the spirit of innocent untroubled country days. Listen, men! Now it is no longer the hot battle cry, but the cool quiet pipe—listen—the forest glens...the hills...the downs, the green sweetness of night.

CARBON: *(Looking at other soldiers who have awakened)* You make them weep.

CYRANO: For homesickness—a hunger more noble than that hunger of the flesh. It is their hearts now that are starving.

CARBON: Yes, but you melt down their manhood.

CYRANO: You think so? There is iron in their blood not easily dissolved in tears.

(DE GUICHE enters.)

DE GUICHE: Good morning!

(All snap to attention.)

CYRANO: Up, up. Christian, get up.

DE GUICHE: What have we here? Black looks?
Yes, gentlemen—I am informed I am not popular;
I can afford your little hates. My conduct under fire is well known. It was only yesterday I drove the enemy backward, pouring my men down like an avalanche;
I myself led the charge.

CYRANO: And your white scarf?

DE GUICHE: You heard that episode? I was in danger of being shot or captured. But, I thought quickly—flung away the scarf that marked my military rank and escaped among my own force. My device was a success.

CYRANO: Possibly. But an officer should not lightly resign the privilege of being a target. Why don't you

lend me your white scarf. I'll lead the first charge
tonight, with it over my shoulder!

DE GUICHE: You are safe making that offer, and you
know it—my scarf lies where I dropped it, on the river
bank between the lines, a spot swept by artillery,
impossible to reach alive!

CYRANO: (*Produces the scarf from his pocket*) Yes. Here...

(DE GUICHE *takes the scarf. General laughter*)

DE GUICHE: Quiet! Thank you. Here is a bit of news
for you: Last night we had hopes of reprovisioning the
army. Under cover of the dark, the marshal moved to
our supply base. He may reach it, but to return safely
he needs a large force—at least half our entire strength.
We have left here merely a skeleton.

CARBON: Fortunately, the enemy does not know that.

DE GUICHE: Oh, yes; they know. My spies tell me they
will attack.

CARBON: Ah! Well, gentlemen!

DE GUICHE: You may have perhaps an hour.

LE BRET: Oh—an hour!

DE GUICHE: The great thing is to gain time.
Any moment the marshal may return.

CARBON: And to gain time?

DE GUICHE: You will all be so kind as to lay down your
lives!

CYRANO: Ah! Your revenge?

DE GUICHE: I make no great pretense of loving you.
But since you gentlemen esteem yourselves invincible—
bravest of the brave and all that, why need we be
personal?

CYRANO: Sir, permit me to offer you all of our thanks.

DE GUICHE: You love to fight a hundred against one; here is your opportunity! Carbon, a word with you.

(He and CARBON *move away.)*

CYRANO: Christian?

CHRISTIAN: Roxane...

CYRANO: Yes.

CHRISTIAN: I should like to say farewell to her, with my whole heart, written for her to keep.

CYRANO: Yes, I know. I thought of that— *(Takes a letter from his pocket)* I have written your farewell.

CHRISTIAN: Show me!

CYRANO: You want to read it?

CHRISTIAN: Of course! *(He takes the letter, begins to read, looks up suddenly.)* What?—

CYRANO: What is it?

CHRISTIAN: Look—this little circle—

CYRANO: *(Takes back the letter quickly)* Circle?

CHRISTIAN: Yes—a tear!

CYRANO: So it is!... Well—a poet while he writes is like a lover in his lady's arms, believing his imagination—all seems true. You understand!

CHRISTIAN: You—wept?

CYRANO: Why, yes—because...it is a little thing to die, but—not to see her...that is terrible! And I shall never—We shall never—You will never—

CHRISTIAN: Give me that! *(Takes letter)*

(Noise in the distance, on the outskirts of camp.)

LE BRET: Halt—who goes there?

CARBON: What is it?—

LE BRET: Why, a coach.

CARBON: What? In the camp? A coach? Coming this way—it must have driven through enemy lines.

RAGUENEAU: *(Offstage)* "On the service of the King".

ROXANE: *(Enters)* Good morning!

DE GUICHE: On the King's service? You?

CHRISTIAN: Roxane!

(Scripted ad-libs, spoken simultaneously, excitement and surprise)

CHRISTIAN: Why have you—

ROXANE: Your war lasted so long!

CHRISTIAN: But why?—

ROXANE: Not now—

DE GUICHE: You cannot remain here!

ROXANE: Why, certainly! Would you believe—they fired at us! My coach looks like the pumpkin in the fairy tale. Oh, you may recognize an old friend!

(RAGUENEAU enters, carrying a basket.)

RAGUENEAU: Gentlemen!

CARBON: Ragueneau!

(Scripted ad-libs, spoken simultaneously)

CYRANO: Ragueneau!

ROXANE: *(To CYRANO)* Cyrano, I am glad to see you!

CYRANO: Oh—how did you come through?

ROXANE: Why, through the enemy lines, of course.

CYRANO: And they let you pass?

RAGUENEAU: Of course! Never underestimate the power of food and drink, and a beautiful woman.

ROXANE: We simply drove along. Now and then
someone scowled at me and I smiled back—my best
smile, dropped my eyes, and said, "I have a lover",
whereupon they let us pass.

CHRISTIAN: But, Roxane—

ROXANE: I know—I said "a lover"—but you
understand—Forgive me!—If I said "I am going
to meet my husband", no one would believe me!

DE GUICHE: You must leave this place.

CYRANO: You must leave. At once.

ROXANE: I?

LE BRET: Yes—immediately.

ROXANE: And why?

CHRISTIAN: Because...

DE GUICHE: This post is dangerous

ROXANE: (To DE GUICHE) Oh—you wish to make a
widow of me?

DE GUICHE: On my word of honor—

ROXANE: No matter. But perhaps you ought to leave us.
Any moment now, there may be danger.

DE GUICHE: You may change your mind—there will yet
be time—

ROXANE: Never!

CHRISTIAN: Roxane!...

ROXANE: No!

DE GUICHE: Very well! (To CARBON) I had one gun
remaining. I have had it placed there— (Pointing off)
—in that corner—for your men. Roxane, you have
time to escape.

ROXANE: No, I stay here.

DE GUICHE: Very well—I stay here also.

ROXANE: Why?

DE GUICHE: Must I run away and leave a woman?

CYRANO: Sir, you show courage!

CARBON: I will place my men, who would long for the sight of you, before they die. Open the hand that holds your handkerchief.

ROXANE: Why?

CARBON: Our company was in want of a banner and have now the fairest in the Army.

ROXANE: Rather small.

CARBON: Lace and embroidered.

DE GUICHE: We'll review them; will you take my arm?

(They go out with CARBON. CHRISTIAN *starts to follow.* LE BRET *speaks with* RAGUENEAU.*)*

CYRANO: Christian!—One moment, I must talk to you before you speak with her.

CHRISTIAN: *(To* CYRANO*)* Speak quickly! What is it?

CYRANO: If Roxane...

CHRISTIAN: Well?

CYRANO: ...speaks about your letters...

CHRISTIAN: Yes—I know!

CYRANO: ...do not make the mistake of showing...

CHRISTIAN: What?

CYRANO: Showing surprise.

CHRISTIAN: Surprise—why?

CYRANO: I must tell you!... It is quite simple I had forgotten it until just now. You have....

CHRISTIAN: Speak quickly!—

CYRANO: You have written oftener than you think.

CHRISTIAN: Oh—have I? For a month we have been blockaded here!—How did you send all these letters?

CYRANO: Before daylight, I managed—

CHRISTIAN: I see. That was also perfectly simple! So I wrote to her, how many times a week? Twice? Three times? Four?

CYRANO: Oftener.

CHRISTIAN: Every day?

CYRANO: Yes—every day...every single day...

CHRISTIAN: And that wrought you up into such a flame that you faced death—

(CARBON *returns with* ROXANE, *then goes back out.*)

CYRANO: Hush—not before her!

(ROXANE *comes up to* CHRISTIAN. CYRANO *sits at a distance.*)

ROXANE: Now—Christian!

CHRISTIAN: *(Takes her hands)* Tell me now why you came here.

ROXANE: Because—your letters...

CHRISTIAN: Meaning?

ROXANE: It was your own fault if I ran into danger! I went mad—mad with you! Think what you have written me.

CHRISTIAN: All this for a few absurd love letters—

ROXANE: Hush—absurd! How can you know? I thought I loved you, ever since one night when a voice that I never would have known, under my window, breathed your soul to me...but—all this time, your letters—every

one was like hearing your voice there in the dark,
all around me, like your arms around me.

CHRISTIAN: So—you came—here.

ROXANE: Oh, my Christian. Oh, my King—lift me up if
I fall upon my knees—it is the heart of me that kneels to
you and will remain forever at your feet—You cannot
lift that!—I came here to say, "Forgive me"—It is time
to be forgiven now, when we may die soon—Forgive
me for being light and vain and loving you only
because you were beautiful.

CHRISTIAN: Roxane!...

ROXANE: It is yourself I love now, your own self.

CHRISTIAN: *(Taken aback)* Roxane!

ROXANE: How you must have suffered, for you must
have seen how frivolous I was; and to be loved for the
poor casual body you went about in—to a soul like
yours, that must have been torture! That image of
you filled my eyes first—I see better now.

CHRISTIAN: Oh!—Roxane!—

ROXANE: I understand: You cannot perfectly believe in
me—a love like this.

CHRISTIAN: I want no love like this! I want love only
for—

ROXANE: Only for what every woman sees in you?
I can do better than that! *(She kisses* CHRISTIAN.*)*

CHRISTIAN: No—it was better before!

ROXANE: Darling, there is more of me than there was.
I had to learn to use my wings. Now, I can love more
of you. If you were less lovable—

CHRISTIAN: No!

ROXANE: —Less charming—ugly even—I should love you still.

CHRISTIAN: You mean that?

ROXANE: I do mean that!

CHRISTIAN: Ugly?...

ROXANE: Yes, even then!

CHRISTIAN: Oh...God!...

ROXANE: What is it?

CHRISTIAN: Only...nothing...one moment...

ROXANE: But—

CHRISTIAN: I am keeping you from our friends—go speak to them.

ROXANE: Dear Christian!

CHRISTIAN: Go—

(She goes to the others.)

CHRISTIAN: Cyrano!

CYRANO: What is wrong?

CHRISTIAN: She does not love me anymore.

CYRANO: You think not?

CHRISTIAN: She loves you.

CYRANO: No!

CHRISTIAN: She loves only my soul.

CYRANO: No!

CHRISTIAN: Yes—that means you. And you love her.

CYRANO: I—

CHRISTIAN: I see—I know.

CYRANO: Yes...I do.

CHRISTIAN: Tell her so!

CYRANO: No.

CHRISTIAN: Why not?

CYRANO: Why—look at me!

CHRISTIAN: She would love me if I were ugly.

CYRANO: She—said that?

CHRISTIAN: Yes. Now then—

CYRANO: Nonsense. Don't believe any such madness. You will never be ugly—go—she would never forgive me.

CHRISTIAN: That is what we shall see.

CYRANO: No—no—

CHRISTIAN: Let her choose between us!—Tell her everything!

CYRANO: No—you torture me—

CHRISTIAN: Shall I ruin your happiness, because I have a cursed pretty face? That seems too unfair.

CYRANO: And am I to ruin yours, because I happen to be born with power to say what I know you feel?

CHRISTIAN: I am tired of being my own rival. I want her love for the poor fool I am—or not at all! I'll know, one way or the other. Now I shall walk down to the end of the post. Go tell her. Let her choose one of us.

CYRANO: It will be you.

CHRISTIAN: God—I hope so! (*He turns and calls.*) Roxane!

CYRANO: No—no—

ROXANE: (*Hurries to him*) Yes, Christian?

CHRISTIAN: Cyrano has news for you—important— (*He goes out.*)

ROXANE: Oh—important?

CYRANO: *(Takes her hand)* Nothing—only Christian thinks you ought to know.... Was it true—what you told him just now?

ROXANE: It was true! I said I should love him even....

CYRANO: The word comes hard—before me?

ROXANE: Even if he were....

CYRANO: Say it—I shall not be hurt!—Ugly?

ROXANE: Even then I should love him.

(Gunshots heard—LE BRET and RAGUENEAU rush out. ROXANE turns to the sound.)

ROXANE: Oh! They are fighting!

CYRANO: Hideous?

ROXANE: Hideous.

CYRANO: Disfigured?

ROXANE: Or disfigured.

CYRANO: Even grotesque? You could love him so?

ROXANE: Yes—and more!

CYRANO: It is true, true. I—Roxane—listen—

LE BRET: *(Rushing in)* Cyrano—

CYRANO: Yes?

LE BRET: Hush!.... *(Whispers a few words to him)*

CYRANO: *(Lets fall ROXANE's hand)* Ah!

ROXANE: What is it?

CYRANO: All gone...

ROXANE: What is it? *(She goes to look offstage.)*

CYRANO: All gone. I cannot ever tell her, now...ever....

ROXANE: What has happened?

(CARBON *and* RAGUENEAU *enter, carrying a body.*
It is CHRISTIAN.)

CYRANO: All gone...

ROXANE: Christian! Christian! Christian!

CARBON: *(To* CYRANO*)* At the first volley. *(He rushes off.)*

CHRISTIAN: Roxane!...

CYRANO: *(Low and quick, in* CHRISTIAN's *ear)* I have told
her; she loves you.

(CHRISTIAN *closes his eyes.)*

ROXANE: *(Turns to* CHRISTIAN*)* Yes, my darling?
(To CYRANO*)* He is not dead?... A letter—over his
heart— *(She opens it.)* For me.

CYRANO: But, Roxane—come away, they are fighting—

ROXANE: Wait a little...he is dead. No one else knew
him but you.... *(She weeps quietly.)* Was he not a great
lover, a great man, a hero?

CYRANO: Yes, Roxane!

ROXANE: A heart deeper than we knew—a soul
magnificently tender?

CYRANO: Yes, Roxane!

ROXANE: He is dead now....

CYRANO: Why, so am I—for I am dead, and my love
mourns for me and does not know....

(Trumpet sounds.)

DE GUICHE: *(Appears)* Our army has returned!

CYRANO: *(To* DE GUICHE*)* Sir, take her away—
I am going—take care of her.

DE GUICHE: As you will—we can win, if you hold on a little longer—

CYRANO: Good!

(Calls to ROXANE, *as she is carried away by* DE GUICHE *and* RAGUENEAU)

CYRANO: Farewell, Roxane! *(He kneels over* CHRISTIAN's *body.)*

LE BRET: Cyrano, we must fight now!

CYRANO: Yes, I will be there. I will fight. I must.

(LE BRET *rushes off.* CYRANO *takes* ROXANE's *lace handkerchief from his pocket and places it over* CHRISTIAN's *heart.)*

CYRANO: I have two deaths to avenge now—Christian's and my own!

(Music begins as CYRANO *picks up* CHRISTIAN's *body and carries it up into the dark. The lights begin to change, taking us to...)*

Scene Two

(A garden)

(Late autumn, leaves falling. LISE *is setting a large chair under a tree.* MARGUERITE *comes out.)*

MARGUERITE: Come inside, Lise, he will be here soon. *(A beat)* It must be ten years that he has come here every Saturday. Oh, more. He will not have eaten anything today. We must offer him something. He is poor. It is difficult to try and help him. He gets so angry. Come in. Roxane has a visitor, De Guiche. He has not been to see her for months.

(ROXANE *and* DE GUICHE *enter.* LISE *gives* ROXANE *her embroidery.)*

ROXANE: Thank you, Lise.

(ROXANE *touches* LISE's *face for a moment.* MARGUERITE *and* LISE *go.*)

DE GUICHE: She takes good care of you?

ROXANE: Yes, she and Marguerite. She came to me when Ragueneau lost his shop. We are...good friends now.

DE GUICHE: And you see Cyrano often?

ROXANE: Every week. My old friend brings me all the news. Every Saturday, under that tree. I wait for him, the hour strikes; then I hear, at the last stroke, his footsteps.

DE GUICHE: And you remain here, cloistered, wasting all that gold—forever in mourning?

ROXANE: Forever.

DE GUICHE: And still faithful?

ROXANE: And still faithful...

DE GUICHE: Have you forgiven me?

ROXANE: I am here. Close to the convent and the good sisters.

DE GUICHE: Was Christian...all that?

ROXANE: If you knew him.

DE GUICHE: Ah? We were not precisely...intimate... And his last letter always at your heart? Fourteen years and you love him still?

ROXANE: Sometimes I think he has not altogether died. His love flows all around me, living.

(LE BRET *appears on the steps.*)

ROXANE: Ah, Le Bret!—How is it with Cyrano?

LE BRET: Badly.

DE GUICHE: Indeed?

ROXANE: Oh, he exaggerates!

LE BRET: Just as I said—Loneliness, misery—I warned him!—He makes a host of enemies—He attacks the false judges, the false saints, the false heroes, the false artists—in short, everyone!

ROXANE: But they fear that sword of his—no one dare touch him.

DE GUICHE: Hmm. That may be so.

LE BRET: It is not violence I fear for him. But solitude—poverty—old gray December stealing into his darkening room.

DE GUICHE: Do not pity him. He lives his own life, his own way—thought, word, and deed free!

LE BRET: Sir!

DE GUICHE: Yes, I know—I have all; he has nothing. Nevertheless, today I should be proud to shake his hand. *(To* ROXANE*)* Pardon me one moment. *(He pulls* LE BRET *to the side.)* It is true that no one dares attack your friend. Some people dislike him nonetheless. The other day such a one said to me: "This man Cyrano may die accidentally".

LE BRET: Thank you.

DE GUICHE: You may thank me. Keep him at home all you can. Tell him to be careful.

LE BRET: Careful! He is coming here. I'll warn him.

DE GUICHE: *(To* ROXANE*)* Goodbye!

ROXANE: I will go with you.

DE GUICHE: It is true I envy Cyrano now and then. Do you know, when a man wins everything in this world, when he succeeds too much—he feels somehow a thousand small displeasures with himself. Not quite remorse but, rather, a sort of vague disgust... The robes of honor, mounting up, step by step, to pride and power, somewhere among their folds, draw after them a rustle of dry illusions, vain regrets.

ROXANE: The sentiment does you honor.

DE GUICHE: Oh, yes...?

RAGUENEAU: *(Enters hurriedly)* Roxane!— *(He sees* LE BRET*)* Oh!—you are here.

ROXANE: First speak to Le Bret for a moment.

RAGUENEAU: But, Roxane—

(She goes out with DE GUICHE, *not hearing him.* RAGUENEAU *comes to* LE BRET.*)*

RAGUENEAU: Listen. She need not know so soon— Listen, I went to see Cyrano just now. As I came near his door, I saw him coming out. I hurried on to join him. At the corner of the street as he passed— Could it be an accident—I wonder!—At the window overhead, someone with a heavy log of wood let it fall—

LE BRET: Cyrano!

RAGUENEAU: I ran to him—

LE BRET: God! The cowards!

RAGUENEAU: I found him lying there—a great hole in his head—

LE BRET: Is he alive?

RAGUENEAU: Alive—yes. But...I had to carry him up to his room.

LE BRET: Is he suffering?

RAGUENEAU: No; unconscious.

LE BRET: Did you call a doctor?

RAGUENEAU: One came—for charity.

LE BRET: We must not tell Roxane all at once....
What did the doctor say?

RAGUENEAU: He said fever and lesions of the—I forget.
Quickly—there is no one to care for him—all alone—
if he tries to raise his head, he may die!

LE BRET: This way—it is shorter.

ROXANE: (*Appears and calls to* LE BRET) Le Bret!—

(LE BRET *and* RAGUENEAU *rush off without hearing.*)

ROXANE: Running away when I call to him? Poor dear
Ragueneau. Must have been very tragic! What a
day!...something in these bright autumn afternoons.
Where was I? Hard sometimes, to match these faded
colors.

(*She sits down with her needlepoint. The clock strikes.*)

ROXANE: The hour!—He will be coming now.

(*As it does,* LISE *and* MARGUERITE *appear, waiting.
The clock strikes six.*)

ROXANE: All done striking? He never was so late before!
Certainly nothing could ever keep him away.

(CYRANO *appears.* MARGUERITE *exits.*)

ROXANE: (*Glancing up*) After fourteen years, late—
for the first time!

CYRANO: Yes, yes—maddening! I was detained by—

ROXANE: Well?

CYRANO: A visitor, most unexpected.

ROXANE: (*Still sewing*) Was your visitor tiresome?

CYRANO: Why, hardly that—inopportune, let us
say—an old friend of mine—at least a very old
acquaintance.

ROXANE: Did you tell him to go away?

CYRANO: For the time being yes. I said, "Excuse me—this is Saturday—I have a previous engagement, one I cannot miss, even for you—Come back an hour from now".

ROXANE: Your friend will have to wait; I shall not let you go till dark.

CYRANO: Perhaps a little before dark, I must go...

(He sits and leans back in the chair and closes his eyes. ROXANE turns, sees LISE.)

ROXANE: Look—somebody waiting to be teased.

CYRANO: *(Opens his eyes)* Of course! Come here, my dear. Beautiful downcast eyes!—So shy—

(LISE sees his face and gasps. He indicates ROXANE.)

CYRANO: Sh!—Careful! I have not eaten anything today! Will you make me a great bowl of hot soup?

ROXANE: You are quite reasonable today! Has Lise tamed you at last?

CYRANO: Yes, she has, now I think of it, that is so—you, bursting with goodness all these years. Astonishing I call it. Ah, now I'll astonish you—I am going to—let you pray for me tonight at vespers!

ROXANE: Aha!

CYRANO: Look at her—awestruck.

(LISE rushes off, away from the house.)

ROXANE: Lise? What can be the matter with her this evening?

CYRANO: *(Quickly interrupting)* Now, may the devil take me, if I ever hope to see the end of that embroidery!

ROXANE: I thought it was time you said that.

(Silence. Leaves fall.)

CYRANO: Look, the leaves—

ROXANE: What color—perfect Venetian red! Look at them fall.

CYRANO: Yes—they know how to die. A little way from the branch to the earth, a little fear of mingling with the common dust, and yet they go down gracefully—a fall that seems like flying!

ROXANE: Melancholy—you?

CYRANO: Why, no, Roxane!

ROXANE: Then let the leaves fall. Tell me now the news.

CYRANO: Let me see—

ROXANE: Ah!

CYRANO: Saturday, the twenty-sixth... *(His eyes close; his head sinks back; silence.)*

ROXANE: *(She goes to him.)* Cyrano!

CYRANO: *(Opens his eyes)* What...what is it?... No—oh no—it is nothing—truly!

ROXANE: But—

CYRANO: My old wound—

ROXANE: My poor friend!

CYRANO: Oh, it is nothing; it will soon be gone... There, it is gone!

ROXANE: We all have our old wounds—I have mine— here...under this faded scrap of writing... It is hard to read now—all but the blood—and the tears....

CYRANO: Christian's letter!... Did you not promise me that some day...that some day...you would let me read it?

ROXANE: His letter... You wish—

CYRANO: I do wish it—today.

ROXANE: *(Gives him the letter)* Here.

CYRANO: May I...open it?

ROXANE: Open it, and read.

CYRANO: *(Unfolds the letter; he reads.)* "Farewell, Roxane, because today I die."

ROXANE: Aloud?

CYRANO: "I know that it will be today, my own dearly beloved—and my heart still so heavy with love I have not told, and I die without telling you! No more shall my eyes drink the sight of you like wine, nevermore, with a look that is a kiss, follow the sweet grace of you—"

ROXANE: How you read it—his letter!

CYRANO: "I remember now the way you have, of pushing back a lock of hair with one hand, from your forehead—and my heart cries out—"

ROXANE: His letter...and you read it so....

(The darkness increases imperceptibly.)

CYRANO: "Cries out and keeps crying: Farewell, my dear, my dearest—"

ROXANE: In a voice...

CYRANO: "My own heart's own—my own treasure..."

ROXANE: In such a voice...

CYRANO: "My love ...

ROXANE: As I remember hearing...long ago...

(She comes near him, softly, without his seeing her, passes the chair, leans over silently, looking at the letter. The darkness increases.)

CYRANO: "—I am never away from you. Even now, I shall not leave you. In another world, I will be still that one who loves you, loves you beyond measure, beyond—"

ROXANE: *(Lays her hand on his shoulder)* How can you read now? It is dark.... *(Takes her hand away)* And all these fourteen years, he has been the old friend, who came to me to be amusing.

CYRANO: Roxane!—

ROXANE: It was you.

CYRANO: No, no, Roxane, no!

ROXANE: And I might have known, every time that I heard you speak my name...

CYRANO: No—it was not I—

ROXANE: It was...you!

CYRANO: I swear!

ROXANE: I understand everything now: The letters— that was you....

CYRANO: No!

ROXANE: And the dear, foolish words—that was you....

CYRANO: No!

ROXANE: And the voice...in the dark...that was...you!

CYRANO: On my honor—

ROXANE: And...the Soul!—that was all you.

CYRANO: I never loved you—

ROXANE: Yes, you loved me.

CYRANO: No—he loved you—

ROXANE: Even now, you love me!

CYRANO: No!

ROXANE: And why...so great a "No"?

CYRANO: No, no, my own dear love, I love you not!...

ROXANE: Why were you silent for so many years?
All the while, every night and every day, he gave me
nothing—you knew that—You knew here, in this letter
lying on my breast, your tears. You knew they were
your tears—

CYRANO: The blood was his.

ROXANE: Why do you break that silence now, today?

CYRANO: Why? Oh, because—

(LE BRET *and* RAGUENEAU *enter, running.*)

LE BRET: What recklessness—I knew it! He is here!

CYRANO: Well? Here I am!

RAGUENEAU: He has killed himself coming here!

ROXANE: Oh, God...and that faintness...was that?

CYRANO: No, nothing! I did not give you the
news—Saturday, twenty-sixth: An hour or so before
dinner, Cyrano de Bergerac died, foully murdered.
(*He uncovers his head and shows it swathed in bandages.*)

ROXANE: Oh, Cyrano!—What have they done to you?—

CYRANO: "Struck down by the sword of a hero, let me
fall—steel in my heart and laughter on my lips!" Yes,
I said that once. How fate loves a joke! Behold me,
ambushed! My battlefield—a gutter. My noble foe
a lackey, with a log of wood!...It seems too logical—
I have missed everything, even my death!

RAGUENEAU: Ah, sir!—

CYRANO: Ragueneau, stop blubbering!

ROXANE: Marguerite!—

CYRANO: No, do not go away—I may not still be here when you return.

(MARGUERITE *enters.*)

ROXANE: You shall not die! I love you!—

CYRANO: No—That is not in the story! You remember when Beauty said "I love you" to the Beast that was a fairy prince, his ugliness changed and dissolved, like magic... But you see I am still the same.

ROXANE: And I—I have done this to you! All my fault—mine!

CYRANO: You? Why no. I had never known womanhood and its sweetness but for you. My mother did not love to look at me—I never had a sister—later on, I feared the mistress with a mockery behind her smile. But you—because of you I have had one friend not quite all a friend—across my life, one whispering silken gown!...

LE BRET: *(Pointing to the moon)* Your other friend is looking at you.

CYRANO: I see....

ROXANE: I never loved but one man in my life, and I have lost him twice....

CYRANO: Le Bret—I shall be up there presently in the moon—without having to invent any flying machines!

ROXANE: What are you saying?...

CYRANO: The moon—yes, that would be the place for me—my kind of paradise! I shall find there those other souls who should be friends of mine—

LE BRET: No! No! No! It is too idiotic—too unfair—such a friend, such a poet—such man to die so—to die so!

CYRANO: There goes Le Bret, growling!

LE BRET: My friend!—

ROXANE: Oh!—

(LISE *returns with the priest.* MARGUERITE *immediately goes to* LISE.)

RAGUENEAU: Cyrano—

CYRANO: Philosopher and scientist,
Poet, musician, duelist—

He flew high, and fell back again!
A pretty wit—whose like we lack—

A lover...not like other men...

Here lies Hercule-Savinien
de Cyrano de Bergerac—

Who was all things—and all in vain!

Well, I must go—pardon—I cannot stay!
My moonbeam comes to carry me away....
(*He raises himself erect and pushes* ROXANE *and the others away, falls to the ground.*) Not here!—Not lying down!...

(*They spring forward to help him; he motions them back.*)

CYRANO: Let no one help me—no one!—only the tree...
It is coming...I feel already shod with marble...gloved
with lead.... Let the old fellow come now! He shall find
me on my feet—sword in hand— (*Draws his sword*)

(*Scripted ad-libs*)

LE BRET: Cyrano!—

ROXANE: Oh, Cyrano!

RAGUENEAU: My friend!

MARGUERITE: Oh, dear God!

CYRANO: I can see him there—he grins—he is looking
at my nose. That skeleton—What's that you say?
Hopeless?—Why, very well!—But a man does not fight

merely to win! No—no, better to know one fights in
vain!...You there—Who are you? A hundred against
one—I know them now, my ancient enemies. *(He lunges
at the empty air.)* Falsehood!... There! Prejudice, there!
—Compromise, there!— Cowardice! There!—
(Thrusting) What's that? No! Surrender? No! Never—
never!... Ah, you too, vanity! I knew you would
overthrow me in the end—no! I fight on! I fight on!
I fight on! *(He swings the blade in great circles, then pauses,
gasping. When he speaks again it is in another tone.)* Yes,
all my laurels you have riven away, and all my roses.
But tonight, when I enter before God, my salute shall
sweep all the stars away from the blue threshold! For
in spite of you, there is one crown I bear away with me.
One thing without stain unspotted from this world,
my own!—And that is...

(He staggers a moment, begins to fall. ROXANE *rushes to
him. He falls into her arms as she sinks to her knees.)*

ROXANE: *(Her mouth to his ear)* And that is...?

CYRANO: My shining soul...

(Music swells and...the curtain falls.)

END OF PLAY

BROADWAY PLAY PUBLISHING INC

ADAPTATIONS OF THE CLASSICS

ALKI (PEER GYNT)

ANYTHING TO DECLARE?

THE BROTHERS KARAMAZOV

A CHRISTMAS CAROL

DEAD SOULS

DON JUAN

DON QUIXOTE DE LA JOLLA

THE FATHER

FIGARO/FIGARO

FRANK LANGELLA'S CYRANO

IL CAMPIELO

THE ILLUSION

JITTERBUGGING: SCENES OF SEX FROM A NEW SOCIETY
(LA RONDE)

MAN OF THE FLESH (DON JUAN)

THE MARRIAGE OF FIGARO

MCTEAGUE: A TALE OF SAN FRANCISCO

PLAYBOY OF THE WEST INDIES

THE PROMISE (THE DYBBUK)

THÉRÈSE RAQUIN

THREE SISTERS

BROADWAY PLAY PUBLISHING INC

ONE ACT COLLECTIONS

BIG TIME & AFTER SCHOOL SPECIAL

THE COLORED MUSEUM

ENSEMBLE STUDIO THEATER MARATHON `84

FACING FORWARD

GIANTS HAVE US IN THEIR BOOKS

ONE ACTS AND MONOLOGUES FOR WOMEN

ORCHARDS

ORGASMO ADULTO ESCAPES FROM THE ZOO

PLAYS BY LOUIS PHILLIPS

ROOTS IN WATER

SHORT PIECES FROM THE NEW DRAMATISTS

**WHAT A MAN WEIGHS &
THE WORLD AT ABSOLUTE ZERO**

BROADWAY PLAY PUBLISHING INC

TOP TEN BEST SELLING
FULL-LENGTH PLAYS AND
FULL-LENGTH PLAY COLLECTIONS

AVEN'U BOYS

THE BROTHERS KARAMAZOV

THE IMMIGRANT

ONE FLEA SPARE

ON THE VERGE

PLAYS BY TONY KUSHNER
(CONTAINING A BRIGHT ROOM CALLED DAY
& THE ILLUSION)

PLAYS BY AISHAH RAHMAN
(CONTAINING THE MOJO AND THE SAYSO,
UNFINISHED WOMEN...,
& ONLY IN AMERICA)

PRELUDE TO A KISS

TALES OF THE LOST FORMICANS

TO GILLIAN ON HER 37TH BIRTHDAY